Mapping Global Cities

GIS Methods in Urban Analysis

Ayşe Pamuk

ESRI PRESS
REDLANDS, CALIFORNIA

ESRI Press, 380 New York Street, Redlands, California 92373-8100

Copyright © 2006 ESRI

All rights reserved. First edition 2006
10 09 08 07 06   1 2 3 4 5 6 7 8 9 10

Printed in the United States of America

Library of Congress Cataloging-in-Publication Data
Pamuk, Ayse.
    Mapping global cities : GIS methods in urban analysis / Ayse Pamuk.
        p.   cm.
    Includes bibliographical references and index.
    ISBN 1-58948-143-7 (pbk. : alk. paper)
    1. City planning. 2. Geographic information systems. I. Title.
    HT166.P333 2006
    307.1'2160285–dc22   2006010177

ISBN-13: 978-1-58948-143-5
ISBN-10: 1-58948-143-7

Ask for ESRI Press titles at your local bookstore or order by calling 1-800-447-9778. You can also shop online at www.esri.com/esripress. Outside the United States, contact your local ESRI distributor.

ESRI Press titles are distributed to the trade by the following:

In North America, South America, Asia, and Australia:
Independent Publishers Group (IPG)
Telephone (United States): 1-800-888-4741
Telephone (international): 312-337-0747
E-mail: frontdesk@ipgbook.com

In the United Kingdom, Europe, and the Middle East:
Transatlantic Publishers Group Ltd.
Telephone: 44 20 7373 2515
Fax: 44 20 7244 1018
E-mail: richard@tpgltd.co.uk

On the cover: "Percentage of foreign-born by census tract" map based on data provided by the U.S. Census Bureau, Census 2000.
Cover and interior design by Savitri Brant

To my mother,
for her love and support,
and for encouraging me to explore cities she has never seen.

Contents

CD contents

About the exercises
Exercise 1   Create a thematic map
Exercise 2   Spatialize nonspatial data
Exercise 3   Analyze vector data
Exercise 4   Analyze raster data
Exercise 5   Calculate new information
Self-directed project: Planning in the new global metropolis

Exercise data

List of figures

List of maps

List of tables

List of abbreviations

ABAG	Association of Bay Area Governments
ACS	American Community Survey
ACSP	Association of Collegiate Schools of Planning
ADB	Asian Development Bank
AESOP	Association of European Schools of Planning
BARD	Bay Area Regional Database
CBD	central business district
CCLI-EMD	Course Curriculum and Laboratory Improvement-Educational Materials Development
CDBG	Community Development Block Grant
COPC	Community Outreach Partnership Centers
CSISS	Center for Spatially Integrated Social Science
CSO	Central Statistical Office
EMF	European Mortgage Federation
ESG	Emergency Shelter Grants
EU	European Union
FGDC	Federal Geographic Data Committee
FMR	fair market rent
GDP	gross domestic product
GIS	geographic information system
GPS	Global Positioning System
HDI	Human Development Index
HLM	habitations a loyer modere
HOME	HOME Investment Partnerships Program
HOPWA	Housing Opportunities for Persons with AIDS
HUD	U.S. Department of Housing and Urban Development
IAURIF	Institut d'Aménagement et d'Urbanisme de la Region d'Île-de-France
IBGE	Instituto Brasileiro de Geografia e Estatistica
INSEE	Institut National de la Statistique et des Études Économiques
IPEA	Instituto de Pesquisa Econômica Aplicada
IPP	Instituto Municipal de Urbanismo Pereira Passos
MAUP	modifiable area unit problem
MSA	Metropolitan Statistical Area
NAFTA	North America Free Trade Agreement
NCGIA	National Center on Geographic Information Analysis
NGO	nongovernmental organization
NSDI	National Spatial Data Infrastructure

NSF	National Science Foundation
OECD	Organisation for Economic Cooperation and Development
OMB	Office of Management and Budget
OUP	Office of University Partnerships
PPGIS	Public Participation GIS
PUMA	Public Use Microdata Area
PUMS	Public Use Microdata Sample
SFSU	San Francisco State University
SOPEMI	Systeme d'Observation Permanente des Migrations
SPOT	Satellite Probatoire d'Observation de la Terre
TANF	Temporary Assistance for Needy Families
TIGER	Topologically Integrated Geographic Encoding and Referencing
UAA	Urban Affairs Association
UCGIS	University Consortium of Geographic Information Science
UNCHS	United Nations Centre for Human Settlements
UNDP	United Nations Development Programme
USAID	U.S. Agency for International Development
USGS	U.S. Geological Survey
UTM	universal transverse Mercator

Acknowledgments

Mapping Global Cities and its accompanying datasets are the result of a multiyear team project. This book would not have been completed without the unfailing encouragement and work of many colleagues, friends, and the remarkable ESRI Press staff. I am grateful to all.

National Science Foundation (NSF) Course Curriculum and Laboratory Improvement-Educational Materials Development (CCLI-EMD) Grant 0228878 provided partial funding for this book project, starting in June 2003. Myles Boylan, program director at NSF, set high professional standards and showed great interest in the successful implementation of the NSF proposal.

Dean Joel Kassiola of San Francisco State University's College of Behavioral and Social Sciences enthusiastically supported the completion of this book and the entire NSF project.

It was a delight to see the book come to life at ESRI Press. Christian Harder was an enthusiastic supporter of the project and provided key guidance in the earliest stages. Judy Hawkins, manager of ESRI Press, provided a team that assisted me in so many ways. David Boyles edited the book and helped resolve many issues along the way. Savitri Brant designed the book and cover. Michael Law, cartographic specialist, helped develop many of the maps for publication and assisted with graphics. Editor Amy Collins put the exercise data through rigorous testing, edited the exercises, and prepared the exercises and data CD for publication. Miriam Schmidts and Shauna Neidigh tested the exercises. Brian Parr and Laura Bowden provided feedback on an early version of the exercises and data and set high standards for the work that followed. Tiffany Wilkerson copyedited the book. Carmen Fye provided critical support by securing the copyright permissions. Lesley Downie provided helpful administrative support. Cliff Crabbe oversaw print production.

The NSF project's principle investigator, Professor Richard LeGates of San Francisco State University, and I worked collaboratively to obtain and administer the grant, identified data sources, organized data, defined concepts to cover, and worked out the research design, review process, training, evaluation, and other aspects of the NSF project. Professor LeGates completed a companion volume, *Think Globally, Act Regionally: GIS and Data Visualization for Social Science and Public Policy Research* (ESRI Press 2005).

A 2003/2004 San Francisco State University President's Fellowship allowed partial release time to focus on this book project and related research projects. The University of California, Berkeley's Institute of Urban and Regional Development provided an intellectual home and a forum to share early results. Professor John Landis, chair of the University of California at Berkeley's Department of City and Regional Planning, provided critical input during the early stages of the conceptualization process during the fall 2003 semester at Berkeley. Professors Karen Chapple and Elizabeth MacDonald of the University of California at Berkeley's Department of City and Regional Planning, and Professor Rolf Pendall of Cornell University, provided exceptionally helpful feedback at our monthly writing group meetings at the women's faculty club at Berkeley during the spring 2004 semester.

Some of the ideas in this book were presented at national and international planning conferences. The research on immigrant clusters was presented at the joint conference of the Association of Collegiate Schools of Planning (ACSP) and the Association of European Schools of Planning (AESOP) in Leuven, Belgium (July 2003); the Urban Affairs Association (UAA) conference in Washington, D.C. (March/April 2004); Johns Hopkins University Urban Fellows Association conference in Padova/Venice, Italy (June 2004); and the ACSP conference in Kansas City (October 2005). Chapter 3 was presented at the Johns Hopkins University Urban Fellows Association conference in Barcelona, Spain (June 2006). Participants at these forums provided helpful suggestions.

Monique Nakagawa, a senior research associate at the San Francisco State University (SFSU) Public Research Institute; Christopher Simeone, an SFSU student with a BA in geography; and Michael Reilly, a PhD candidate in city and regional planning at the University of California at Berkeley, provided invaluable assistance in gathering and cleaning the data, editing the maps, assisting with the exercises, and providing feedback on early versions. I greatly appreciated their hard work and good humor.

SFSU students Jody Littlehales (Master of Public Administration), Aly Pennucci (Urban Studies), Frederick Schermer (Urban Studies), Bridgette Carroll (Urban Studies), Michael Doherty (Urban Studies), and the 2004 Urban Studies Senior Seminar class students enthusiastically tested draft versions of the exercises and applied what they learned to assist three of the 2004 Urban Studies Senior Seminar class clients: the San Francisco Planning Department, Excelsior Neighborhood Commercial Revitalization, and the Northeast Community Federal Credit Union.

Ten faculty colleagues beta tested an early version of the exercises during a summer workshop (July 12–18, 2004) at SFSU, and some of them used the materials in their own universities and classrooms in fall 2004. These faculty are Haydar Kurban (Howard University, Economics), Sanda Kaufman (Cleveland State University, Urban Studies), Francis Neely (San Francisco State University, Political Science), Mary Edwards (University of Illinois, Urbana-Champaign, Urban Planning), John Flateau (Medgar Evers College, CUNY, Public Administration), Gianpaolo Baiocchi (University of Massachusetts, Amherst, Sociology), Xinhao Wang (University of Cincinnati, City Planning), XiaoHang Liu (San Francisco State University, Geography), Christopher Bettinger (San Francisco State University, Sociology), Mai Nguyen (San Francisco State University, Urban Studies).

Diane Godard of the San Francisco State University Public Research Institute has developed the plan for evaluating the instructional module and evaluated the July 2004 version of the exercises at SFSU and other universities.

Many other faculty colleagues and friends around the world provided helpful suggestions during the proposal development process in spring 2002, including Qing Shen (University of Maryland) and Zorica Nedovic-Budic (University of Illinois, Urbana-Champaign), and generously sent spatial data in 2003/2004, including Fernando Cavallieri (Instituto Municipal de Urbanismo Pereira Passos, Rio de Janeiro), Monica Haddad (Iowa State University), Mariette Sagot, (Institut d'Amenagement et d'Urbanisme de la Region d'Îlle-de-France, IUARIF, Paris), and Rinus Deurloo and Sako Musterd (University of Amsterdam). Anne Shlay (Temple University) provided helpful comments on chapter 4.

The following people deserve thanks for sharing photographs or data used in the book: Michael Donovan (University of California, Berkeley); Scott Edmondson, AnMarie Rodgers, and Jasper Rubin (San Francisco Planning Department); Myron Orfield and Aaron Timbo (Ameregis); Jeff Johnson (San Francisco Department of Telecommunications and Information Services), and Larry Orman (GreenInfo Network).

Andrew Roderick, Alex Keller, Vincent Cheung, Barry Nichols, Lena Deng, and the rest of the extraordinary SFSU Behavioral and Social Sciences technical support staff maintained the servers and networks and kept ArcGIS software running smoothly in our offices and computer labs.

Corrado Poli and Tulin Erdem provided close friendship, support, and inspiration during the long period of this book's writing.

Any errors that remain are, of course, mine.

Ayşe Pamuk
San Francisco, California
June 2006

Introduction

Advances in transportation and telecommunications technology coupled with the globalization of economic activities have resulted in voluntary and involuntary uprooting of populations in search of better futures. Urban planners and policy analysts, particularly in global metropolitan regions, have often been caught unprepared to deal with the new challenges unleashed by international and domestic migration patterns worldwide. The influx of immigrants[1] into *global cities*[2] or *global city-regions*[3] such as San Francisco, Los Angeles, New York, Amsterdam, and Paris, and dramatic demographic transformations in these areas, now require rethinking conventional approaches to meeting new urban management challenges. The internal rural exodus fueling urban growth in *megacities*[4] in the developing world, such as Rio de Janeiro, presents another set of challenges.

Spatial thinking and analysis are essential for intelligent urban policymaking in a globally connected world. Without a spatial and analytical understanding of how cities are organized and how residential patterns are shaped as a result of population and employment changes, we risk designing urban plans and policies that are unrealistic at best, and exclusionary for newcomers at worst. Geographic information systems (GIS) can be usefully applied by planners to new urban planning challenges in these global metropolitan regions and megacities, especially those where rapid demographic transformations are primarily responsible for recent rapid growth. The analysis of relevant data with GIS can provide a powerful new perspective in addressing urban research and policy questions, and holds the potential to deepen our collective understanding and efforts in solving important urban policy problems.

Mapping Global Cities is driven by my long-standing desire to understand the evolution of human settlements throughout the world. My interest in the housing conditions of the urban poor began in the early 1980s in Ankara, Turkey. While studying city and regional planning at the Middle East Technical University, I observed first-hand the conditions of impoverished populations living in informal housing settlements.[5] Having experienced a comfortable childhood in Izmir, a port city on the west coast of Turkey, I was struck by how the "other half" of the population lived and became curious about uneven urban development. Later, during my master's and PhD studies in city and regional planning at the University of California at Berkeley, my theoretical interest in human settlements deepened, and my quest led me to undertake field research on land and housing markets and policy in Trinidad and Tobago. While teaching urban planning at the University of Virginia in the late 1990s, I did fieldwork research in Brazil, a result of my interest in human settlements in the developing world.

Today, as an associate professor of urban studies at San Francisco State University, I draw upon this international background and work, blend my experience in the so-called first- and third-world settings, and extend it in new ways by using the power of spatial analysis with GIS. The discussion of GIS methods in this book draws significantly from my own research in the areas of housing and urbanization in developing nations, spatial distribution of poor children and child-care provision in San Francisco, and immigrant clusters in U.S. and European global cities. Along with Professor Richard LeGates's companion book, *Think Globally, Act Regionally* (2005), this book seeks to inspire other social scientists to use GIS in urban research and to integrate spatial thinking and analysis into quantitative methods courses.[6]

The types of localities I am concerned with in this book—global metropolitan regions—have volatile population growth trajectories largely caused by migration, especially international migration patterns. The main questions addressed in this book are the following: What spatial commonalities and differences exist in major metropolitan areas where immigrants are located? Where do immigrants settle in specific global metropolitan regions? What is the level of concentration and density of different immigrant groups in these areas? Are there commonalities in immigrant clustering patterns among different global cities? Are these patterns similar when analyzed at different scales? What is the incidence of traditional ethnic *enclaves* (e.g., Chinatowns in urban core areas of the United States)? What is the incidence of contemporary ethnic communities in the suburbs? How is the concentration of immigrants in certain areas in metropolitan regions related to housing and labor market dynamics? What processes seem to explain the formation, change, and persistence of ethnic enclaves and communities in global cities?

Mapping Global Cities also addresses my desire to better understand how spatial relationships affect the lives of different population groups, especially those living in poverty with limited locational choices. So I ask the following questions: Are poor children located disproportionately in certain areas of the urban core rather than others? How can the isolation of poor families in high-poverty metropolitan neighborhoods be eradicated? What public policies are necessary to increase access of poor families with children to social services such as child care and early childhood education?

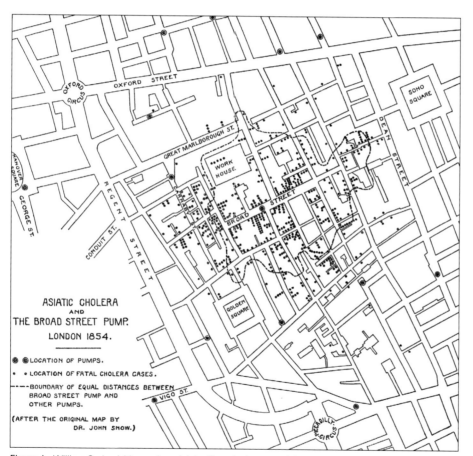

Figure i   William Sedgwick's version of John Snow's dot map of deaths during a cholera outbreak in London's Soho district, 1854.

Source: Gerstein Science Information Centre, University of Toronto.

The use of GIS in urban mapping

On the importance of using spatial analysis in urban research, historians frequently refer to the pioneering work of John Snow, a London-based physician who mapped deaths from cholera during the epidemic in 1854. His mapping of deaths as points in London's Soho neighborhood revealed clustering of cholera outbreaks around a public drinking water standpipe as the source of infection—the famous Broad Street pump. Snow's original map was modified to communicate different intentions by many mapmakers (Koch 2005). Figure i shows one of these maps: William T. Sedgwick's 1911 adaptation of Snow's 1855 map of the Broad Street epidemic. Sedgwick—a professor of sanitary science and public health in Boston—drew attention to the boundary of equal distances between the Broad Street pump and other pumps in Snow's maps. The location of fatal cholera cases in relation to the Broad Street pump helped illustrate the waterborne reality of the bacterium that causes cholera. Sedgwick used this adaptation of Snow's map to illustrate proven methods of sanitary science—a branch of public health (Koch 2005). Other more recent adaptations of Snow's map were published by Edward E. Tufte (1983, 24) in his *The Visual Display of Quantitative Information* and by Mark Monmonier (1996, 158) in his *How to Lie with Maps*.

Mapping by Ernest W. Burgess, a pioneer sociologist at the University of Chicago in the 1920s, and the development of the entire field of social ecology, are other important

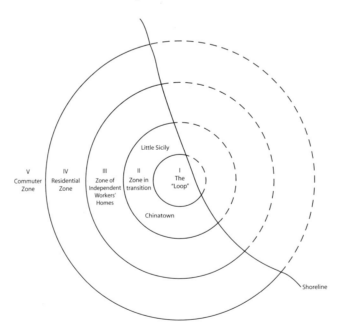

Figure ii Concentric zones, Chicago School, 1925.

Source: Derived from Ernest W. Burgess and Roderick McKenzie, "The Growth of a City: An Introduction to a Research Project." In *The City*, eds. Robert E. Park and Ernest W. Burgess (Chicago, Ill.: University of Chicago Press, 1925).

milestones in urban mapping. The spatial clustering among immigrants (discussed in chapters 5 and 6), for example, was first noted by Chicago School sociologists who observed this phenomenon during the course of their research focusing on Chicago's neighborhoods in the 1920s. The human ecology approach states that cities develop through a process of competition for space that ultimately gives rise to homogenous concentric zones (Burgess 1925). According to this theory, new ethnic groups are first expected to live in congested conditions in *zones-in-transition* areas but move to working-class districts soon after their socioeconomic situation improves. The concentric zone map *(figure ii)* is one of the first attempts to visually represent the spatial organization of cities and to highlight the tendencies of cities to expand radially from their central business districts (CBDs)—in Chicago, for example, this area is called the Loop. As figure ii shows, the ethnic neighborhoods of Little Sicily and Chinatown are adjacent to Zone I—the downtown area (CBD). Burgess labeled this area Zone II and called it "zone-in-transition"—the area where business and light manufacturing are located. Zone III included workers who escaped the zone-in-transition area (II) but wanted to live close to work. The residential zone (Zone IV) consisted of apartment buildings occupied by higher-income households and single-family housing districts. The commuter zone (Zone V) is beyond the city limits, about thirty to sixty minutes away from the CBD, and includes suburbs comprised of single-family homes (Burgess 1925).

In his writings, Burgess describes forces of invasion and succession and depicts the transformation of cities as a dynamic and organic process guided by these forces. The concentric zone maps were drawn in Chicago, but were soon extrapolated to (and imposed upon) many other cities by other urban ecologists, sometimes quite inappropriately.

Real estate economist Homer Hoyt analyzed residential patterns in 142 cities and found that the rent structure of housing was organized by sectors (e.g., along transportation corridors), not concentric zones. In the 1930s, Hoyt used this analysis to develop his sectoral model, an alternative to Burgess's concentric zone theory. Other alternatives to the concentric zone theory included the multiple nuclei model developed by geographers Chauncy Harris and Edward L. Ullman in the 1940s. Since then, many urban scholars have developed theories about the spatial organization of cities, but none was as influential as the urban ecology approach developed by the Chicago School of sociologists. The concentric zone images were so powerful that they influenced how urban researchers imagined the spatial organization of cities thereafter.

GIS technology was developed in the early 1960s, spurred by pioneering work by the Canadian Land Inventory in 1963 and the establishment of the first academic GIS lab at Harvard University in 1964. Since then, a broad area of application has been developed (Longley et al. 2005). Human, health, and social services is a growing area for GIS applications (Haithcoat et al. 2001). Local government agencies and community-based organizations increasingly use public domain data from federal agencies like the U.S. Census Bureau to carry out demographic analyses of local areas, which accelerates the process of making data available to everyone (democratization) (Sawicki and Craig 1996). Such studies support planning, policy formulation, management, and delivery of social services. Tabular census data coupled with administrative data from human services agencies can now be relatively easily transformed into geographically referenced spatial data for display and analysis in GIS. GIS is particularly useful in analyzing census and other geographic data spatially and in solving public policy problems with a spatial component (Budic 1994; O'Looney 2000; Greene 2000). Public sector agencies and community-based organizations use these tools more and more often to monitor neighborhood indicators such as crime rates, house values, rents, and demographics.

Gathering the data and preparing it for spatial analysis are the most time-consuming and expensive aspects of GIS analysis (discussed in chapter 2). Many agencies and organizations have established regional data centers and disseminate frequently used local data on the Internet. The Association of Bay Area Governments (ABAG), for example, makes spatial data on San Francisco Bay Area jurisdictions available on the Internet for urban planning applications. Many university-community partnership centers funded by the U.S. Department of Housing and Urban Development (HUD) have established urban data centers that have empowered community groups who undertake their own analyses of data, and encouraged public participation in local planning. A network of policy analysts and academics using GIS in community-oriented projects convene at an annual Public Participation GIS (PPGIS) conference. HUD has made the Community 2020 CD package—GIS software bundled with demographic and administrative data—available to local governments nationwide to permit GIS analysis in the preparation of Consolidated Plan[7] documents required for federal funding of local housing and community development programs. The uniform nationwide format of the census data coupled with sector-based program data (e.g., location and demographics of public-housing projects), when made available in this way from a federal agency like HUD or regional agency like ABAG, is tremendously helpful for agencies that otherwise do not have resources to undertake expensive data organization and maintenance activities. Data standardization efforts by the National Spatial Data Infrastructure (NSDI) and others hold the potential to ultimately improve public access to high-quality spatial data and increase use of GIS in urban planning and policy analysis.

Another example of urban mapping widely known among urban planners is Myron Orfield's "Metropolitics" maps, which show metropolitan inequalities in taxes, schools, and availability of public services (Orfield 2002). These types of analytical maps are tremendously valuable for metropolitan planning agencies and policymakers. Using data from 4,606 incorporated municipalities and 135 unincorporated areas in twenty-five U.S. metropolitan regions, Orfield has created a system for classifying communities using two broad categories:

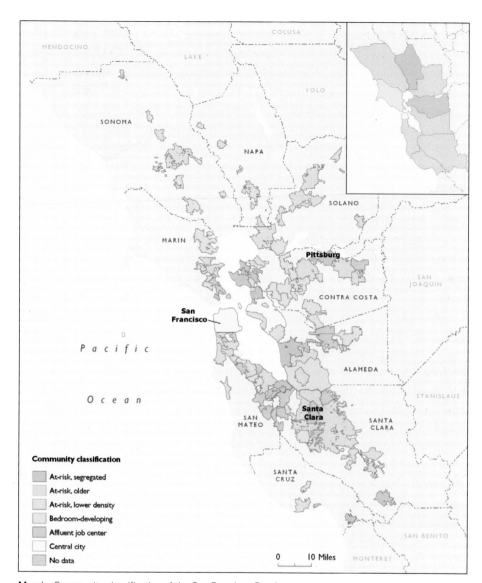

Map i   Community classification of the San Francisco Bay Area.

Data sources: San Francisco Community Classifications.; Myron Orfield, *American Metropolitics: The New Suburban Reality* (Washington, D.C.: Brookings Institute Press, 2002).

tax capacity and costs. Tax capacity is measured using two variables: (1) 1998 tax capacity per household; and (2) the growth in tax capacity between 1993 and 1998. Cost is measured by four variables: (1) percentage of elementary students eligible for the free or reduced-price lunch program in 1997; (2) 1998 population density; (3) population growth between 1993 and 1998; and (4) the age of the housing stock in 1990 (Orfield 2002, 31).

Orfield's analysis of the data has revealed five types of communities across the United States: (1) at-risk, segregated communities; (2) at-risk, older communities; (3) at-risk, low-density communities; (4) bedroom-developing communities; and (5) affluent job centers. Map i shows where these communities are located in the San Francisco Bay Area. Not surprisingly, Santa Clara, the heart of the Silicon Valley, is classified as an affluent job center. Pittsburg, a suburb of San Francisco, is classified as an at-risk, segregated community. As we shall see later, areas near Pittsburg also contain a concentration of Philippines-born immigrants (discussed in chapters 5 and 6). Orfield's maps are a good example of displaying the results of data analysis and how the classification operations of GIS software are effectively used to display results of analysis on maps. His mapping efforts cover twenty-five U.S. metropolitan regions and piece together hard-to-find, high-quality local data, such as numbers of elementary school students eligible for free or reduced-price lunch programs. As such, the maps are a significant contribution to the regional planning literature.

This book's spatial analyses of immigrant population concentrations and clusters in four U.S. metropolitan regions seek to broaden our understanding of how such people congregate in some of the world's most densely populated places. Visualizing the spatial organization of cities and metropolitan regions has become far easier as GIS software has become easier to use. Technological advances have the potential to push the theoretical envelope (from the 1920s Chicago School concepts to today's understanding of community typologies) as researchers can analyze larger datasets and display the results in maps created using GIS. In addition to increasing our theoretical understanding of the spatial organization of cities, GIS also solves many different types of public policy problems.

The distinction between a scholarly interest in physical space and a pragmatic interest in solving public policy problems with a spatial component is a useful one to make at this point. In the former, spatial analysis methods are employed to answer particular research questions such as residential clustering patterns of different immigrant groups in cities (Pamuk 2004; Beveridge 2002), spatial segregation patterns (Wong 2003), historical redlining in mortgage lending (Hillier 2003), and in building urban forecasting and simulation models (Landis and Zhang 2000; Shen 2004). Urban planning professionals, city managers, and policy analysts mainly employ the pragmatic type of spatial analysis methods and focus on pressing public policy problems such as the concentration of preschool-age children in high-poverty neighborhoods (discussed in chapter 4). Other urban mapping applications include seismologists using GIS to identify areas prone to earthquakes, epidemiologists using GIS to identify areas of high incidence of disease (Koch 2005), environmental scientists using GIS to identify ecologically vulnerable areas for protection, and transportation planners using GIS to identify commute patterns in metropolitan areas (Bailey and Gatrell 1995).

Both types of knowledge generation are of course valuable, and creative and relevant work for bettering cities is more likely to flourish at the intersections of theory and practice. Spatial analysis tools can sometimes open up new understandings that are not otherwise apparent by providing new ways of processing data for researchers and practitioners alike. While some in the social sciences work with inherently spatial questions, the use of spatial analysis methods has not been widespread among them. The relative accessibility of spatial analysis tools and advances in computing technology now make it possible to display, analyze, and model social phenomena that have a spatial component. As geographers Trevor C. Bailey and Anthony C. Gatrell put it, "the recognition of a spatial dimension in analysis may yield different, and more meaningful, results, than an analysis which ignores it" (Bailey and Gatrell 1995, 6).

On the educational front, a large group of scholars and educators have defined this rapidly growing field of spatial analysis as geographic information science and technology, emphasizing its functionality and usefulness for spatial data handling and analysis (University Consortium for Geographic Information Science 2003). Over the last decade a network of National Science Foundation–funded geographers in the United States organized under the umbrella of the National Center on Geographic Information Analysis (NCGIA) have developed materials for a core curriculum in geographical information science and a list of questions that GIS can answer (NCGIA 2000; Nyerges and Golledge 1997). Another National Science Foundation grant has funded the Center for Spatially Integrated Social Science (CSISS) at the University of California, Santa Barbara, in 1998 (Goodchild and Janelle 2004). A national group of geographers, engineers, and planners has developed model curricula for geographic information science and technology under the umbrella of University Consortium for Geographic Information Science (University Consortium for Geographic Information Science 2003). Several major publishers have devoted significant resources to disseminating this knowledge to broader audiences; these include ESRI Press books on GIS, the Prentice Hall series on GIS, and the Francis and Taylor GISDATA series.

Organization of the book

Mapping Global Cities is organized into three parts. Part I provides an overview of core GIS concepts used in specific public policy applications and in analyzing research questions in parts II and III. The intended audience has a global outlook and a special interest in understanding the evolution of contemporary cities and regions in the context of late twentieth and early twenty-first century globalization. An important element of this framework has to do with international migration movements and resulting location of immigrants in certain global city-regions and in certain areas (suburbs and central cities) in these regions. As contemporary metropolitan areas fundamentally change, spatial analysis with GIS provides us with a powerful new perspective in empirically and visually analyzing these changes.

Building on the foundation developed in part I (including key GIS concepts and data), the next two sections of the book focus on GIS applications that deal with specific public policy and research questions. Part II deals with urban planning and social service delivery. Part III addresses locating immigrant clusters in global cities and an analysis of housing conditions in areas where immigrants live. The book includes a CD with five short exercises and a self-directed project demonstrating how GIS concepts are put into practice with ArcGIS software. The datasets used in the exercises are all high-quality data from U.S. and international sources. The same datasets were used to produce the maps in the chapters. Readers can replicate the analyses on their own for the same areas or for other geographic locations. Main sources of public domain spatial data available on the Internet are introduced in chapter 2.

Readers with different interests and GIS experience may use this book differently. *Mapping Global Cities* aims to reach different audiences. The data and substantive matter contained in the six hands-on exercises included in the CD are closely connected to discussions in the chapters and provide readers immediate access to GIS analysis tools with international and U.S. data. I invite readers to jump in and start using the datasets to follow along with the research questions I have been enthusiastically pursuing as part of my own research program. Expand and elaborate further on these and other questions as data permits. Data dictionaries are included on the CD for variables highlighted in the exercises and additional variables.

My hope is that *Mapping Global Cities* will be widely used by urban studies and planning students studying policy analysis, housing policy, and international development, as well as data analysis. International development professionals, human settlement experts in the developing world, and urban planning practitioners working in immigration gateway regions of the United States, Europe, and the developing world may also find the book useful. This book may also appeal to researchers and scholars concerned with housing and human settlements policy analysis throughout the world.

I anticipate many readers of this book will already be familiar with introductory GIS concepts and operations. For excellent introductions to fundamental GIS concepts see Michael N. DeMers's *Fundamentals of Geographic Information Systems* (2005), Keith C. Clarke's *Getting Started with Geographic Information Systems* (2003), and Paul A. Longley et al.'s *Geographic Information Systems and Science,* second edition (2005). Operations in ArcGIS software are covered in Ormsby et al.'s *Getting to Know ArcGIS Desktop,* second edition (2004). For an introduction to cartography see Borden D. Dent's *Cartography: Thematic Map Design,* fifth edition (1999), and Terry A. Slocum et al.'s *Thematic Cartography and Geographic Visualization* (2005).

Think Globally, Act Regionally (LeGates 2005), mentioned previously, is an excellent resource and companion volume to this book. Some familiarity with statistical analysis also would be helpful to readers of *Mapping Global Cities*, but is not required.

Now, I invite you to begin reading the chapters and working through the GIS exercises on the CD as you join me in using GIS as a tool to understand the spatial organization of global cities.

Notes

1   Immigrants are foreign-born persons.

2   The concept of global cities goes back to the theory of world cities developed by Hall (1966) and Friedmann and Wolff (1982). Saskia Sassen's work on global cities (1991) focusing on London, New York, and Tokyo spawned renewed interest in global cities research in the 1990s. See Davis (2005) and Samers (2002) for a review of the global cities research literature. For a collection of classic social science writings about global cities, see Brenner and Keil's anthology: *The Global Cities Reader* (2006).

3   Allen Scott (2002) has defined global city-regions as those areas of the world functioning as important "spatial nodes of the global economy" both in advanced industrialized countries and in the developing world. The concept builds on the pioneering concepts of world cities (Hall 1966; Friedmann and Wolff 1982) and global cities (Sassen 1991), and additionally considers the urban governance structures (e.g., regional planning institutions) and multination institutional arrangements (e.g., NAFTA, OECD, and EU).

4   The United Nations defines megacities as cities with a population above 8 million. Most of these cities are located in developing nations.

5   Informal housing settlements are widespread in developing countries and have four broad features: (1) lack of land tenure security; (2) lack of basic infrastructure such as piped drinking water inside dwelling units, sewerage, and electricity; (3) predominance of physically substandard dwellings; and (4) locations that are not in compliance with land-use regulations and are often not suitable for development (e.g., hillsides, wetlands, floodplains). Informal housing settlements are called *gecekondus* in Turkey, *favelas* in Brazil, *kampungs* in Indonesia, and *bidonvilles* in former French colonies.

6   See the "Space, Culture, and Urban Policy Project" Web site (bss.sfsu.edu/nsfgis/index.htm) at San Francisco State University for additional resources.

7   A Consolidated Plan is a document that outlines a vision for community development actions in local jurisdictions for a three-to-five-year period and covers the use of funds received annually in grants and loans from the U.S. Department of Housing and Urban Development (HUD). Since 1995, it is an application required for funding under the federal Community Planning and Development formula grant programs: Community Development Block Grants (CDBG), HOME Investment Partnerships Program (HOME), Emergency Shelter Grants (ESG), and Housing Opportunities for Persons with AIDS (HOPWA).

Part **1**

Exploring global metropolitan regions with GIS

Chapter *1*

Using GIS to analyze cities in a global world

Quantitative methods are a part of everyday language among social scientists working in research-based disciplines like economics, sociology, political science, public administration, and urban studies.[1] Several subfields within these disciplines, such as urban economics, urban sociology, housing and community development, and land-use planning, are concerned with physical space. And yet, at present, the use of spatial analysis methods in these fields to answer research questions with a spatial component is limited to a small group of researchers concerned with locational models (Harris and Batty 2001), spatial clustering of ethnic groups (Logan and Zhang 2004), housing and mortgage finance (Can 1998), urban activity and forecasting models (Landis and Zhang 2000), and urban growth and land-use policy simulation models (Landis 2001). Spatial analysis methods using GIS have not yet become integrated into the standard methods toolbox of all social scientists. This chapter discusses spatial analysis methods in relation to conventional nonspatial social science quantitative methods to illustrate how GIS can add value to research and should be adopted by those not yet fluent with these methods.

Research in the social sciences

The three main purposes of research in the social sciences are exploration, description, and explanation (Babbie 2001, 91). At present, most urban planning and policy applications of GIS fall under exploratory and descriptive analyses. When researchers have an interesting idea they usually begin with exploratory analysis, which involves reading the relevant literature to identify unanswered research questions. Once an unanswered research question is identified, descriptive research can be carried out with the appropriate methods. Explanatory research goes deeper in an effort to show cause-and-effect relationships and to dissect underlying processes at work. This type of research attempts to develop a plausible model of the phenomenon being studied in order to come up with explanations and predictions for the future based on model assumptions. Today, explanatory research that involves modeling and predictions of some future outcome with spatial data are carried out by researchers with some level of difficulty, even by those with advanced GIS skills. Such loosely coupled models that require exporting data back and forth between GIS software and a statistical software package are cumbersome to create and even harder to replicate (Wong 2003). (Chapters 5 and 6 discuss this type of modeling effort with immigrant clusters data for four global metropolitan regions in the United States.) Developers of GIS software are moving toward adding functionality to handle explanatory research with spatial data solely within the GIS environment, potentially making such analyses and explanations far easier.

Units of analysis

To undertake social science research one has to define the unit of analysis appropriate for the research question at hand. Units of analysis are elements researchers examine to summarize descriptions of all similar elements in order to make generalizations and draw attention to differences among them (Babbie 2001, 95). Frequently the unit of analysis is the same as the unit of observation. In GIS the unit of observation is spatial (e.g., municipality, census tract). Using GIS one can analyze the variation of a phenomenon (e.g., median household income) across space measured and recorded for a particular spatial unit of analysis (e.g., census tract).

Consider the arguments of global city researchers (Sassen 1991; Fainstein 2002) and development economists (Sen 1999) who have long been concerned with inequalities in income and power across the world. That there are significant inequalities in the world should come as no surprise to readers of this book; but how can we measure and communicate such inequalities? And what is the appropriate unit of analysis? International development institutions have created various measures to monitor the well-being of people in different countries. One widely used indicator is the Human Development Index (HDI). The United Nations has been in charge of constructing the HDI since 1990 for each country to measure average achievements in three basic dimensions of human development: (1) life expectancy at birth; (2) educational attainment as measured by adult literacy rate and school enrollment ratio; and (3) standard of living as measured by gross domestic product (GDP) per capita. This composite index (which ranges from 0 to 1) is then used to rank countries. Those with an HDI of 0.800 and above are considered to have high human development. Those countries in the 0.500 to 0.799 range have medium human development, and those below 0.500 are considered to have low human development (United Nations Development Programme 2003; United Nations Centre for Human Settlements 2001). A researcher concerned with the variation of HDI worldwide would use country as the unit of analysis. Those interested in the variation within a particular country, say Brazil, can use Brazilian states or municipalities (a smaller unit of analysis) to analyze the spatial distribution of HDI in Brazil. In essence, research questions drive the selection of the appropriate unit of analysis.

Map 1.1   States of Brazil with São Paulo and its 645 municipalities highlighted.

Data sources: Instituto Brasileiro de Geografia e Estatistica (IBGE)—Brazilian Census Bureau; Instituto de Pesquisa Economica Aplicada (IPEA), www.ipea.gov.br.

Map 1.1 shows Brazil's twenty-seven states and one of its state's (São Paulo's) 645 municipalities. When aggregation of spatial units of analysis at different geographies is possible (e.g., municipalities can be aggregated to states), the smallest available geographic unit of analysis (e.g., municipalities) is usually preferred because it provides a geographically more detailed level of analysis. The Brazil census data displayed on the map comes from Instituto Brasileiro de Geografia e Estatistica (IBGE)—Brazilian Census Bureau, and Instituto de Pesquisa Econômica Aplicada (IPEA) *(www.ipea.gov.br)*.

Similarly, when working with U.S. census data, the ideal unit of geographic observation is the smallest geographic unit for which the desired data is available (e.g., census blocks). For many researchers this is an appropriate choice for unit of analysis. For data collection purposes the U.S. Census Bureau has divided the entire country into uniform geographic areas. At the top of the hierarchy is the geographic area called the Metropolitan Statistical Area (MSA). Each MSA is divided into counties. Each county is divided into census tracts with an average population of 4,000 people. For example, in 2000, there were 176 census tracts in San Francisco. Each census tract is divided into census block groups containing about 1,000 people. In 2000, there were 574 block groups in San Francisco. Nationwide, each census block group is divided into blocks containing about 400 people. This is the smallest geographic level for which the U.S. Census Bureau reports information collected from residents of all known addresses in the country. In 2000, there were 5,792 blocks in San Francisco. This is the finest-grained depiction of census data available for some variables like income by race and Hispanic origin; however, some other variables like the foreign-born population and China-born population are reported only down to the census tract level (discussed in detail in chapter 5) for various reasons, including the requirement to protect the confidentiality of residents. Figure 1.1 shows the U.S. Census geography hierarchy, using the San Francisco area as an example.

The U.S. Census Bureau collects data for other geographic units. One of these is Public Use Microsample Areas or PUMAs, which are larger than census tracts comprised of about 100,000 people. In 2000, the city and county of San Francisco had seven PUMAs *(map 1.2)*. The U.S. Census Bureau provides disaggregated household-level PUMS data for PUMAs, which is very useful for analyzing research and policy questions for which the appropriate unit of analysis is the household (rather than, for example, the census tract).

The U.S. Census data used in this book comes from two main sources: (1) the short-form questionnaire administered by the U.S. Census Bureau in April 2000, which is a 100 percent count of people who were reached on Census Day (April 1, 2000); (2) the long-form questionnaire administered by the U.S. Census Bureau at the same time, which gathers additional information on the financial characteristics of households (e.g., income). This information is gathered from a sample of households (one in six households) from each census block. The 100 percent count data is available in the census data file called SF1, and the sample data is available in the census data file called SF3. The data files used in the exercises have been organized using these names (discussed in chapter 2, table 2.2). Additional variables can be accessed and downloaded from the U.S. Census Bureau's American FactFinder Web site *(factfinder.census.gov)*.

Figure 1.1   The U.S. Census geography hierarchy.

Data source: U.S. Census Bureau, Census 2000 TIGER/Line data.

Map 1.2   PUMAs in the San Francisco Bay Area.

Data source: U.S. Census Bureau, Census 2000 TIGER/Line data.

In France, the smallest spatial unit available to analyze census data is called a *commune*. Map 1.3 shows inner suburbs *(petite couronne)* of Paris (Hauts-de-Seine, Seine-Saint-Denis, and Val-de-Marne) and outer suburbs *(grande couronne)* of Paris (Seine-et-Marne, Yvelines, Essonne, and Val d'Oise), along with the numerous small communes throughout the region. The data and the shapefile come from Institut National de la Statistique et des Études Économiques (INSEE) and Institut d'Aménagement et d'Urbanisme de la Region d'Île-de-France (IAURIF) in Paris.

Communes geographically fit within *départements*. Paris is one of eight départements that make up the Paris metropolitan region, administratively called Île-de-France (Gaubert et al. 1996, 271). Paris itself is divided into twenty communes. The inner suburban ring areas (petite couronne) have seen rapid growth in the 1960s and 1970s at high residential densities. These areas include single-family dwellings mixed with high-rise structures. Large tracts of less-attractive land were developed in the 1970s by the French government known as HLM (*habitations à loyer modéré*—low-rent dwellings) with large blocks of flats (Hall 1977, 60). Neighborhoods and housing units in the older suburbs (in the west) are well-maintained. Suburbs in the north and east, on the other hand, have large concentrations of substandard housing. These areas are heavily populated by immigrants.

Map 1.4 shows foreign-born population in the Paris metropolitan region (Île-de-France) down to the commune level. Pincetl (1996) reported large immigrant population concentrations in northern suburbs of Paris. Indeed, the analysis of the most recent census data (March 1999) shows concentrations of foreigners in spatially contiguous communes in the northern sections of Paris (communes 2, 10, 18, and 19), and along a wide band spanning across petite couronne from central Paris to the north. Maps 1.5 and 1.6 show concentrations of Algerians and Moroccans, respectively.

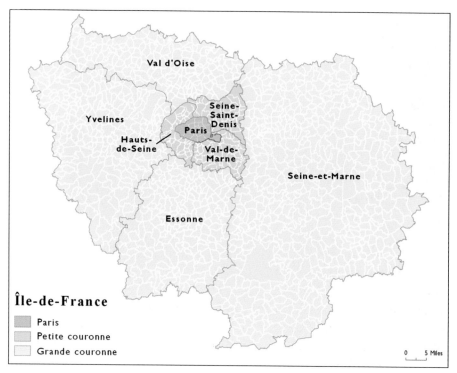

Map 1.3 Départements and communes in the Paris region.

Data source: Atlas des Franciliens, tome 3, 2002 © IAURIF-INSEE.

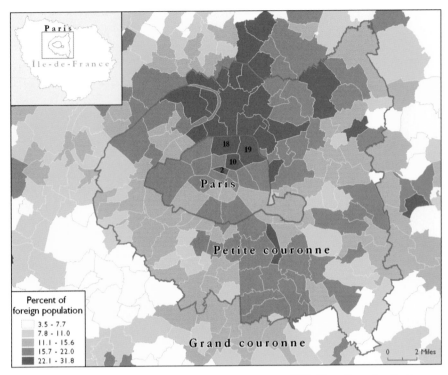

Map 1.4   Percent of foreigners in the Paris region by commune, 1999. (Note: Data classified by natural breaks method. White indicates no data.)

Data source: Atlas des Franciliens, tome 3, 2002 © IAURIF-INSEE.

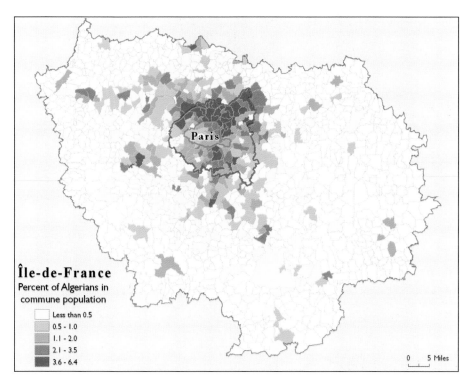

Map 1.5   Immigrant concentrations in the Paris metropolitan region for Algerians by percent of commune population, 1999. (Note: Data classified manually. White indicates no data.)

Data source: Atlas des Franciliens, tome 3, 2002 © IAURIF-INSEE.

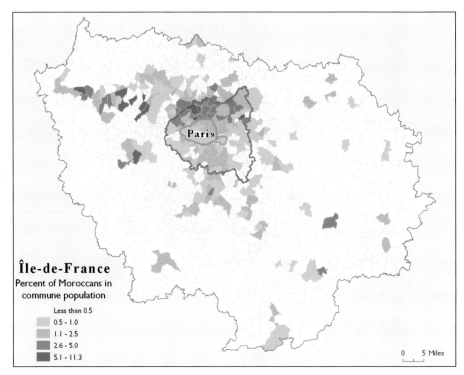

Map 1.6 Immigrant concentrations in the Paris metropolitan region for Moroccans by percent of commune population, 1999. (Note: Data classified manually. White indicates no data.)

Data source: Atlas des Franciliens, tome 3, 2002 © IAURIF-INSEE.

Measurement of variables

The appropriate application of statistical operations to data requires paying close attention to the level of measurement for each of the variables in the dataset. Numerical data is measured quantitatively as nominal-categorical, ordinal, or on an interval-ratio scale (Healey 2002, 10–16). Variables measured at the interval-ratio level can be used to perform mathematical operations to create new variables (e.g., median income per census tract, median house value per census tract). For example, one can create a simple housing affordability indicator for each census tract in the study area by dividing median house value by median household income. A high value for this indicator (greater than 3) indicates low affordability (discussed in chapter 2, map 2.1).

Nominal and ordinal measurements classify cases into categories. Frequencies or percentages for each category can be calculated from nominal and ordinal measurements. One can create a ranking system, which involves recoding (or reclassifying) variables (e.g., low presence, medium presence, and high presence) and calculating the counts (or percentages) using the new categories. Using this information, for example, one can create a bar chart showing the level of concentration of foreign-born population (low, medium, high) in four metropolitan areas *(figure 1.2)*. The Los Angeles MSA, for example, has a larger percentage of its census tracts with medium and high concentrations of foreign-born than the other three metropolitan areas. On the other hand, Los Angeles ranks fourth in the relative numbers of census tracts with low concentrations of foreign-born. These calculations are easily handled in a statistical software package like SPSS software as well as in ArcGIS software.

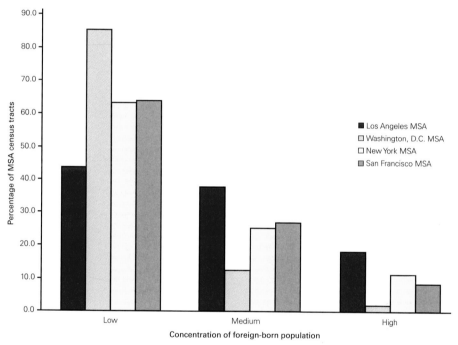

Figure 1.2   Levels of concentration of foreign-born population in census tracts by major U.S. metropolitan regions, 2000.

Data sources: U.S. Census Bureau, Census 2000 Summary File 3 (SF 3), foreign-born population variable (PCT19001); Census 2000 TIGER/Line data down to the census tract level.

Types of spatial data

Urban planners and policy analysts who routinely work with numerical data are very familiar with processing numbers using spreadsheet programs like Microsoft Excel or statistical software packages like SPSS. This data is typically nonspatial. In contrast, GIS is specifically designed to work with spatial data, which means that numerical data is georeferenced to a particular location on earth that can be displayed on a map. In GIS the feature attribute table and the map that stores geographic features are dynamically linked to each other with a common field (feature identifier), which locates the geographic feature on the map. GIS works with two types of spatial data: vector data and raster data *(table 1.1)*. Parts I and III of this book (and exercises 1, 2, 3, 5, and the self-directed project) focus on GIS analysis with vector data. Part II of the book (and exercise 4) illustrates applications using raster data as it adds a powerful dimension to vector data analysis.

	Vector data representation	Raster data representation
Focus of model	Discrete features with precise shapes and boundaries	Continuous phenomena and images of the earth
Main sources of data	Aerial photography GPS receivers Digitized from paper maps Vectorized from raster data	Aerial photography Imaged from a satellite Scanned from blueprints, photos Rasterized from vector data
Spatial storage	Points stored as x,y coordinates Lines stored as paths of connected x,y coordinates Polygons stored as closed paths	Cells (grids)
Geographic analysis	Map overlay Buffering, adjacency, and proximity Polygon dissolve and overlay Spatial and logical query Address geocoding	Spatial coincidence Proximity Surface analysis
Cartographic output	Best for drawing the precise shape and position of features	Best for presenting images and continuous features

Table 1.1   Modeling in GIS.

Source: Michael Zeiler, *Modeling Our World: The ESRI Guide to Geodatabase Design* (Redlands, Calif.: ESRI Press, 1999).

Vector data. The three types of geographic objects that GIS uses to simplify and symbolize the world—points, lines, and polygons—altogether are known as vector data *(figure 1.3)*. The vector data format is suitable when working with discrete variables. A discrete variable has a basic unit of measurement that cannot be subdivided (Healey 2002, 10). For example, population per city is a discrete variable. The basic unit is population. The cities of the world can be represented as points on a world map where the attributes of each city (e.g., population) have discrete values (e.g., 8 million). If measured accurately, there cannot be 8 million and one-half people since people are measured in whole numbers.

Raster data. The second main type of spatial data is known as raster, which is essentially a matrix of identically sized cells (e.g., squares) also known as grids *(figure 1.4)*. Each cell stores values for each of the variables associated with that particular raster grid. In GIS there are two types of grids: continuous and discrete. A continuous grid stores values for a continuous variable (with decimal places), which has a basic unit of measurement that can

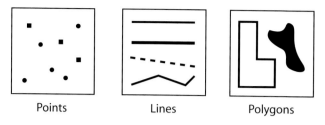

Points   Lines   Polygons

Figure 1.3 Vector data: points, lines, and polygons.

theoretically be subdivided infinitely. Healey (2002) gives the example of time, which can be measured in nanoseconds or a smaller unit (e.g., 10.7 seconds or 10.732451 seconds). Continuous variables are sometimes rounded off and reported as if they are discrete variables. In the GIS environment one can build a surface to represent the continuous distribution of data (e.g., elevation) in space. Each raster grid holds a value that corresponds to a specific range in elevation and is assigned different shades of gray *(figure 1.4)*. One can also work with discrete grids (e.g., grids that store discrete values for demographic group categories). We will work with discrete grids in identifying a suitable location for a new child-care center in chapter 4 and exercise 4.

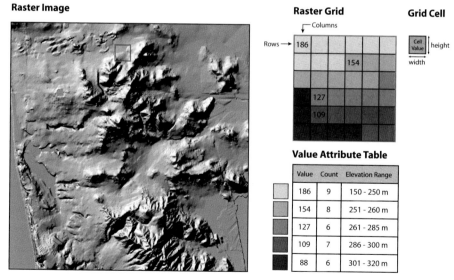

Value Attribute Table

Value	Count	Elevation Range
186	9	150 - 250 m
154	8	251 - 260 m
127	6	261 - 285 m
109	7	286 - 300 m
88	6	301 - 320 m

Figure 1.4 Raster data: grid cells.

Data source: USGS, San Francisco Bay Area Regional Database.

Scale of analysis

When displaying geographically referenced data one needs to pay special attention to the scale of analysis. Maps at different scales can reveal different levels of detail for the same phenomenon. An analysis of the spatial distribution of the foreign-born population focusing on the city and county of San Francisco alone, for example, would overlook major concentrations in the suburbs of the surrounding counties *(map 1.7)*. As we shall see in chapter 6,

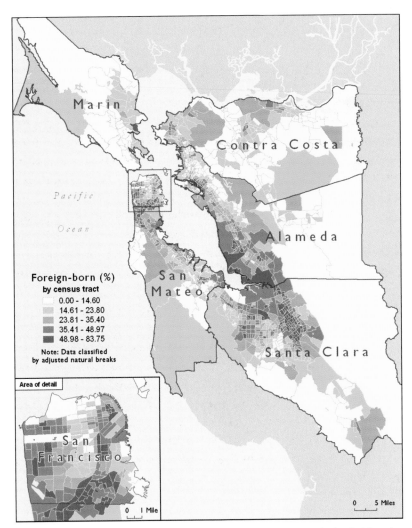

Map 1.7   Scale of analysis: percentage of foreign-born by census tract in the San Francisco Bay Area, 2000.

Data sources: U.S. Census Bureau, Census 2000 Summary File 3 (SF 3), foreign-born population variable (PCT19001); Census 2000 TIGER/Line data down to the census tract level.

immigrant clustering patterns look different when analyzed at the county level, and they reveal somewhat different patterns when compared to results from a regional level analysis.

Basic GIS methods of analysis and software functionality

Most frequently used GIS methods of analysis rely on several basic functionalities of GIS software. These are querying, classifying spatial data in thematic mapping, and symbolizing geographic features. Types of GIS analyses, on the other hand, include single-layer analysis, multilayer analysis, and the analysis of spatial patterns.

Querying

Querying is a form of exploratory analysis in GIS that allows the computer user to inter-actively obtain information about geographic features displayed on the computer screen. It is the most accessible and simplest GIS function. For example, a child-care center is represented on the computer screen as a point. The neighborhood (area) where the center is located is understood by GIS as a polygon. Each of these geographic features (centers as points, neighborhoods as polygons) has attribute data tables associated with it. One can then obtain enrollment statistics for each of the centers by pointing to and clicking a point (center) on the screen. As in a spreadsheet or database system, the GIS querying function allows the user to search for records that meet a certain criteria. For example, a social service provider can query the GIS database to show the nearest child-care centers to beneficiary homes. The query result would show the location of the center on the computer screen. The querying ability of a well-designed GIS can provide significant cost savings in answering citizen inquiries by social service agencies (O'Looney 2000, 15).

Two basic categories of querying in GIS involve the location of features and attributes of features. Map 1.8 was generated by querying the attributes of features (cities) and shows cities in Africa and parts of the Middle East (for which data is available from the UN) where at least one in ten children does not reach 5 years of age. The attribute table shows the population rank class (POP_CLASS) of some of the cities displayed on the map along with the percentage of children who die before reaching their fifth birthday (UND5MORT). Of all the cities that met these criteria, cities in Niger stand out with one in four children not reaching 5 years of age.

Classifying spatial data in thematic mapping

Once compiled, geographically referenced data can be displayed using different classification methods and symbols to display information in map layers. The selection of an appropriate

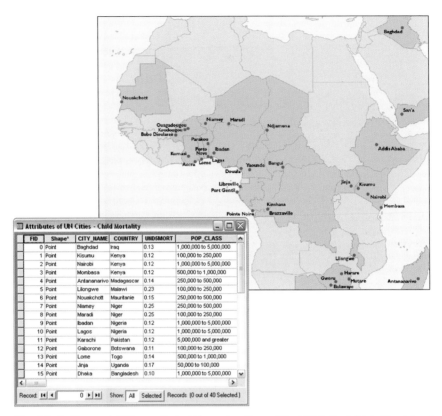

Map 1.8   Incidence of child mortality in Africa and portions of the Middle East. (Note: The dataset contains 125 variables for 232 cities worldwide.)

Data source: United Nations Centre for Human Settlements (UN-HABITAT), global urban indicators data. Global Urban Observatory, 1998.

classification method for the variable at hand involves first exploring the distribution of the data (e.g., in a histogram). To visualize policy-relevant groupings one needs to define breakpoints manually. The federal poverty threshold (discussed in chapter 4) is a good policy-relevant breakpoint to use in classifying poverty data when analyzing the spatial distribution of poor children. Similarly, to locate concentration of China-born people in San Francisco one needs to define breakpoints manually to identify census tracts with China-born population certain percentage points above the MSA level (discussed in chapter 5 and exercise 5). Making breakpoints used in GIS correspond to policy-relevant thresholds such as the federal poverty line is essential for GIS analysis to produce results useful for policy.

Map 1.9 is an example of a thematic (e.g., choropleth) map, which shows the median household income in San Francisco down to the block group level for the year 2000. Darker shades indicate higher income areas. Darkest areas on map 1.9 show San Francisco's census tracts with a median household income of above $100,000. The color ramp comes

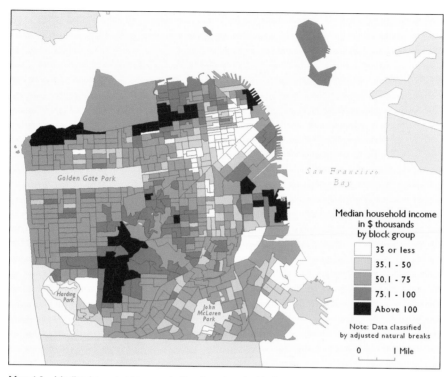

Map 1.9   Median household income in San Francisco by block group, 2000.

Data sources: U.S. Census Bureau, Census 2000 Summary File 3 (SF 3), median household income variable (P053001); Census 2000 TIGER/Line data down to the census block group level.

from ColorBrewer *(www.ColorBrewer.org)*—a National Science Foundation–supported online tool offering color schemes for thematic mapping (Brewer 2005). Thematic mapping involves mapping of feature attribute characteristics (e.g., census variables like median household income). By far the most popular use of GIS is in creating thematic maps like map 1.9. Selecting appropriate data display techniques as well as scale of analysis is important in achieving clarity of communication to facilitate decision making.

Symbolizing spatial data for map display

All attributes associated with points or polygons need to be given a meaning using map symbols. Mapping different levels of concentrations of phenomena (e.g., a specific demographic group, overcrowding, endangered species) is useful for social scientists and urban planners who are concerned with understanding, improving, or protecting the spatial distribution of such phenomena. For example, urban planners who are concerned with improving housing conditions for immigrants in cities can design targeted programs after identifying areas

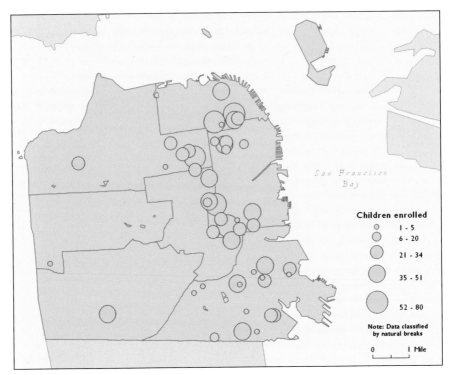

Map 1.10 Locations of Head Start centers and capacity in San Francisco, 2001.

Data source: San Francisco Head Start Program at San Francisco State University, 2001.

where overcrowding (a measure of poor-quality housing) are disproportionately present in high immigrant areas. This would require displaying two variables on the same GIS map together. Exercises 5 and the self-directed project on the CD include census data to analyze overcrowding in San Francisco, New York, Los Angeles, and Washington, D.C.

Symbolizing points. The location of features (e.g., the locations of Chinese-owned businesses) or the attributes of features (e.g., the number of employees in Chinese-owned businesses) could reveal quite different patterns. Map 1.10 shows Head Start center locations (points), and the size of the points indicates the capacity in each center (operating at full capacity) as measured by the number of enrolled children. Notice that most of San Francisco's Head Start centers are located in the city's eastern neighborhoods (discussed in detail later in chapter 4).

Symbolizing areas. Different concentrations of features (geographic objects in a layer such as a census tract) can be represented in choropleth maps. It might be useful to show, for example, where the highest concentrations of China-born census tracts are located in San Francisco. It is also possible to depict the concentration of a phenomenon by mapping the location of features (e.g., in dot density maps); but when there are many features in a small geographic area it might not be easy to see the distribution very clearly. In constructing multiple density maps for comparison purposes a uniform areal unit should be used (e.g., square miles or kilometers).

Map 1.11 is a choropleth map that shows the concentration of people living in *favelas* in the state of Rio de Janeiro, Brazil. Notice that the city of Rio de Janeiro has a medium-high concentration of favela residents (12.1 to 25 percent of municipality population). Favelas in Brazil, like in other developing nations, have grown as a result of rapid urban growth rates in major cities coupled with low urban management capacity to meet housing demand. For many low-income households who cannot afford to purchase or rent formal housing, favela neighborhoods offer an affordable alternative for shelter. One such favela is Rocinha *(figures 1.5 and 1.6)*. With a population of about 200,000 inhabitants, Rocinha is Latin America's largest favela settlement. The denser area toward the bottom of the hill on figures 1.5 and 1.6 is a neighborhood known as Bairro Barcelo. The tree-lined area on the top of the hill is Vila Verde.

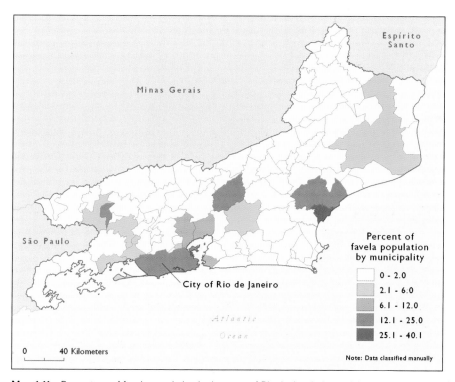

Map 1.11   Percentage of favela population in the state of Rio de Janeiro's municipalities.

Data sources: Instituto Brasileiro de Geografia e Estatistica (IBGE)—Brazilian Census Bureau; Instituto de Pesquisa Economica Aplicada (IPEA), www. ipea.gov.br.

Figure 1.5   Rocinha favela in Rio de Janeiro.

Source: Michael Donovan, 2005.

Figure 1.6   Rocinha favela in Rio de Janeiro.

Source: Michael Donovan, 2005.

Such settlements are called *gecekondus* in Turkey *(figure 1.7)*. Gecekondu literally means "built overnight" in Turkish. By the late 1990s more than half of the population in three of Turkey's largest cities lived in gecekondu settlements: 70 percent in Ankara; 55 percent in Istanbul; and 50 percent in Izmir (Pamuk 1996). Informal housing settlements are widespread in other parts of the world as well. Figures 1.8, 1.9, 1.10 show informal housing in Trinidad (Pamuk 2000). International lending and aid agencies sometimes refer to these settlements as "slums," despite the negative connotation of the word. The UN-HABITAT has recently undertaken a study to estimate the magnitude of "slums" worldwide, and the World Bank has launched a major initiative to create "Cities without Slums" *(www.worldbank. org/urban/upgrading/without.html)*.

Figure 1.7   Gecekondu housing near Izmir, Turkey.

Source: Ayse Pamuk, 1996.

Figure 1.8   Informal housing in Trinidad.

Source: Ayse Pamuk, 1993.

Figure 1.9   Informal housing in Trinidad.

Source: Ayse Pamuk, 1993.

Figure 1.10   Informal housing in Trinidad.
Source: Ayse Pamuk, 1993.

Households living in poverty are disproportionately located in informal housing settlements in the state of Rio de Janeiro as in other major cities of the developing world. Map 1.12 shows the concentrations of poor children in the state of Rio de Janeiro. The city of Rio de Janeiro has 10 to 14 percent of its children living in poverty. In rural areas of the state the percentage of children living in poverty is much higher—22.1 to 31.5 percent. Child poverty is evident even in the developed world. Map 1.13 shows the concentrations of children in poverty in San Francisco (discussed in detail later in chapter 4). Maps 1.12 and 1.13 are thematic maps. As mentioned above, one can also display data analyzed at densities per square mile (O'Looney 2000, 124). Map 1.14 shows children living in households below the federal poverty line in San Francisco per acre, which provides a more accurate depiction of the data (discussed in detail later in chapter 2).

Single-layer analysis

Thematic mapping such as the choropleth maps above can involve a single layer or multiple layers. Single-layer analysis involves working with one variable at a time. Univariate descriptive statistics such as measures of central tendency (mean) and measures of dispersion (standard deviation) are statistics reported for individual variables. The attribute table in GIS where attribute values for each of the geographic features is stored is in essence a

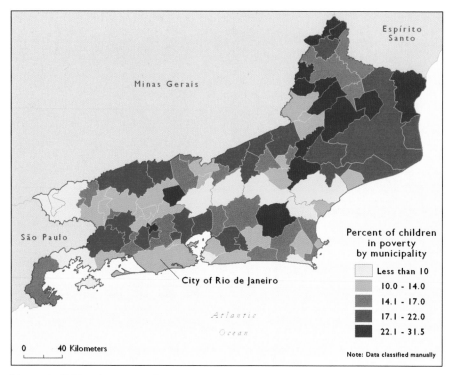

Map 1.12   Children in poverty in Rio de Janeiro, Brazil.

Data sources: Instituto Brasileiro de Geografia e Estatistica (IBGE)—Brazilian Census Bureau; Instituto de Pesquisa Economica Aplicada (IPEA), www.ipea.gov.br.

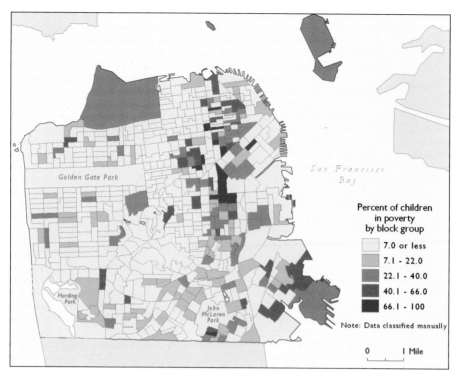

Map 1.13 Percentage of children in poverty in San Francisco by block group, 2000.

Data sources: U.S. Census Bureau, Census 2000 Summary File 3 (SF 3), children in poverty variable (P087003); Census 2000 TIGER/Line data down to the block group level.

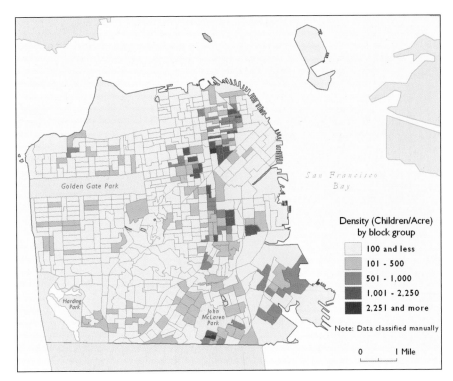

Map 1.14   Children in poverty per acre in San Francisco, 2000.

Data sources: U.S. Census Bureau, Census 2000 Summary File 3 (SF 3), children in poverty variable (P087003); Census 2000
TIGER/Line data down to the block group level.

spreadsheet. The data can be analyzed in a statistical software package like SPSS *(www.spss.com)* outside of the GIS environment. At present, the GIS environment provides limited functionality for statistical data manipulation.

The strength of the GIS environment, of course, is that the attribute table is linked to geographic features (e.g., polygons, points, lines) on the map. As we saw in map 1.8, the points (cities) on the map are linked to an attribute table. One can map variables to show the spatial distribution of that particular variable. Displaying more than one variable in GIS requires working with symbology carefully in order to avoid crowding the map with too many symbols.

Multilayer analysis

Mapping a single variable (e.g., Hispanic children under 5 living in poverty in San Francisco) is informative, provides useful information, and communicates the information simply and powerfully. More often than not, though, handling more than one criterion (variable) is required for decision making. Figure 1.11 shows the concept of multiple vector data layers being used to identify overlapping areas. The layer at the top shows Head Start center locations in San Francisco. The next layer shows concentrations of children under 5 living in poverty. The next layer shows half-mile buffers around Head Start centers. The layer at the bottom shows census block groups. The vertical line that cuts across all four of these layers indicates that the layers are perfectly aligned and have the same map projection system. The combined layer shows the areas where children living in poverty and half-mile buffers overlap in space. These areas are well-served by existing centers. Darker shaded areas on the poverty layer outside of the buffer zones are underserved and represent potential locations for new centers.

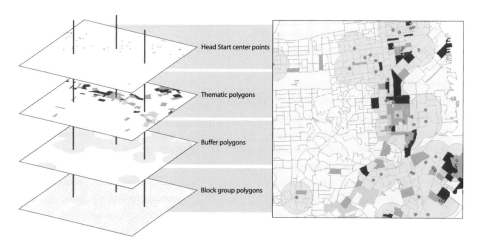

Head Start center points

Thematic polygons

Buffer polygons

Block group polygons

Figure 1.11   Cartographic overlay with vector data.

An early user of the cartographic overlay method was Ian McHarg, a landscape architect whose work spawned the school of thought concerned with environmental sensitivity analysis (McHarg 1969). In pre-GIS days, McHarg worked with transparent acetates. He stacked layers of acetate—each representing a separate variable. Then he put the stack on top of a bright light source, which enabled him to identify the lightest areas penetrating the stack of layers. He determined these areas as most suitable for locating a power line—the focus of his analysis. This method is frequently used by environmental planners working with raster data for environmental suitability analysis. Other decision-making criteria in vector or raster format can also be stacked on top of one another in, for example, facilities siting analyses.

Visualizing more than one variable on a map requires skill and care in communicating the information without overwhelming the audience. Displaying two variables (using two different geographic features) on the same map involves working with one data frame in GIS and two data layers. Map 1.15 shows concentrations of poor Hispanic children under 5 years of age in San Francisco (polygons) and Head Start centers (points). This is known as the point-in-polygon analysis, and it is helpful when one wants to locate two variables at the same geographic area. These are two data layers in the same data frame in GIS. One method of displaying two variables using the same type of geographic feature (polygon) clearly is to change the transparency level of one of the variables. Map 1.16 shows elevation in San Francisco and house values of $500,000 or greater together using the transparency function. Notice that most census tracts with expensive houses in San Francisco are located on higher elevations and likely have commanding views of the San Francisco Bay. Map display techniques for more than one variable are useful when working with both vector and raster data. However, for more sophisticated analysis of numerical data contained in the data layers (e.g., involving multiple factors/variables), one needs to work solely in the raster environment (discussed in chapter 4 and demonstrated in exercise 4).

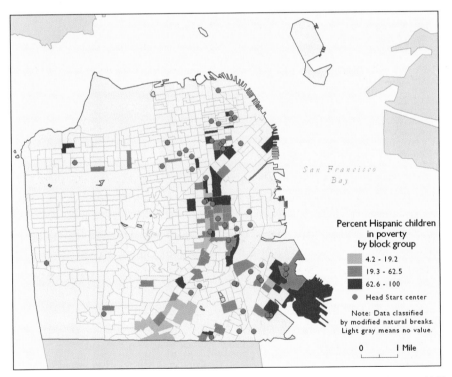

Map 1.15   Head Start centers and Hispanic children in poverty in San Francisco by block group, 2000.

Data sources: U.S. Census Bureau, Census 2000 Summary File 3 (SF 3), Hispanic children in poverty variable (P159H003); Census 2000 TIGER/Line data down to the block group level.

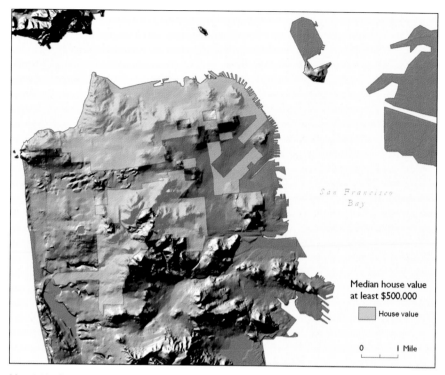

Map 1.16   Raster map of San Francisco and house values, 2000.

Data source: USGS, San Francisco Bay Area Regional Database.

Analysis of spatial patterns

Geographic features in space are distributed in one of three ways: clustered, random, or uniform *(figure 1.12)*. Random distribution does not have a recognizable pattern, while the other two do exhibit a certain type of pattern. One can detect these patterns using dot density maps or choropleth maps. Map 1.17 shows China-born clusters in four U.S. metropolitan regions using a choropleth (shaded area) map, discussed in chapter 6. Map 1.18 shows the China-born population in the San Francisco Bay Area as a dot density map.

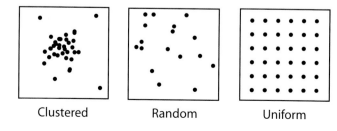

Figure 1.12   Point distribution patterns.

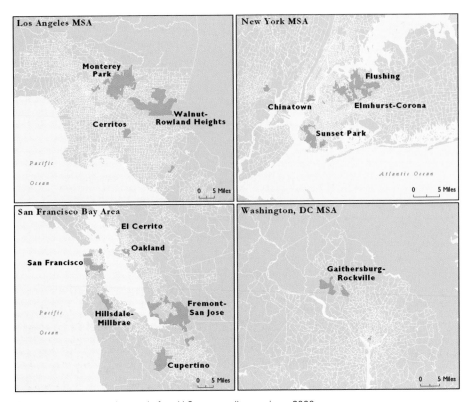

Map 1.17   China-born clusters in four U.S. metropolitan regions, 2000.

Data sources: U.S. Census Bureau, Census 2000 Summary File 3 (SF 3), China-born population variable (PCT19034); Census 2000 TIGER/Line data down to the census tract level.

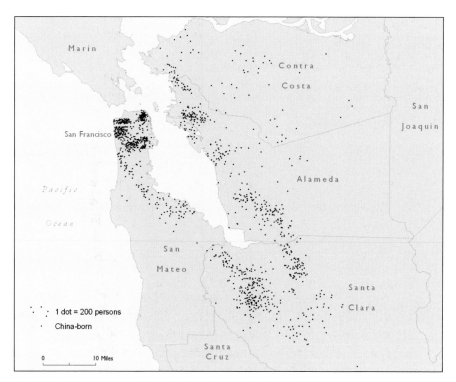

Map 1.18   China-born population in the San Francisco Bay Area, 2000.

Data sources: U.S. Census Bureau, Census 2000 Summary File 3 (SF 3), China-born population variable (PCT19034); Census 2000 TIGER/Line data down to the census tract level.

This chapter discussed fundamental GIS concepts and methods that social scientists concerned with global cities and their regions are most likely to find useful. These methods are applicable anywhere in the world as long as high-quality and appropriate spatial data is available for the type of research questions at hand. The next chapter will discuss sources of spatial data, issues of data quality and reliability, and the challenges of working with U.S. and international data.

Notes

1   For a review of quantitative methods and statistics see these widely used and excellent text-books: *Statistics: A Tool for Social Research*, seventh edition, by Joseph F. Healey (2005), *Social Statistics for a Diverse Society*, fourth edition, by Chava Frankfort-Nachmias and Anna Leon-Guerrero (2006), and *The Practice of Social Research*, tenth edition, by Earl Babbie (2004).

Chapter **2**

Spatial data

Up-to-date and accurate data is crucial for informed public sector decision making. For urban planners and policy analysts, high-quality data makes solid and sophisticated urban analysis possible. For citizens, reliable and easy-to-use population and housing data increases the possibility of full and engaged participation in community planning activities in neighborhoods. Above all, data collection, analysis, and reporting activities are mandated by legislation for the proper implementation of government programs. For all these reasons, there is a substantial amount of information available for urban analysis and planning that has already been collected by federal, state, regional, and local government agencies, international organizations, the private sector, and nonprofit organizations.

This chapter provides an overview of major types of spatial data frequently used in spatial analysis with GIS, main sources of spatial data for urban planning and urban policy analysis, issues related to data quality, and metadata. The chapter will focus on policy-relevant data on population and housing and international data on human settlements. Readers whose research focuses on other subjects like transportation planning, environmental planning, regional planning, or land-use planning should consult comprehensive lists of data sources in their own specialty areas. A good starting point is Yen and York's (2003) comprehensive

International data sources

Cities Data Book. The Urban Indicators for Managing Cities Program of the Asian Development Bank (ADB) tracked urban conditions and trends in eighteen cities in the Asia and Pacific region. The ADB has included cities in the data book that give a cross-sectional view of the types of cities emerging in the region. The 140 indicators range from population and settlement to health and education to municipal services to governance. Matthew S. Westfall and Victoria de Villa, eds., 2001. *Cities Data Book: Urban Indicators for Managing Cities.* Manila, Philippines: Asian Development Bank. *www.adb.org/Documents/Books/Cities_Data_Book/default.asp*, accessed June 2003.

UN-HABITAT Global Urban Indicators Data. The United Nations Centre for Human Settlements (UN-HABITAT) Global Urban Observatory program regularly collects urban indicators in a sample of cities worldwide in order to report on progress in shelter and urban development. Local and national urban observatories as well as selected regional institutions collect the data. Thirty indicators and nine qualitative sources of information are used to measure performances and trends in twenty selected policy areas. These efforts are aimed at tracking progress in the implementation of the Habitat Agenda. Quantitative indicators include land price-to-income ratio, the price of water, and the rate of unemployment. Qualitative data include the level of documentation on housing rights and the availability (or lack thereof) of local environmental plans. *unchs.org/programmes/guo/guo_indicators.asp*, accessed July 2003.

Housing Indicators Program Data. The Housing Indicators Program is a joint program of the United Nations Centre for Human Settlements (UNCHS) and the World Bank. An extensive survey was conducted in fifty-two cities on six continents to assess the housing sector and its economic and social impacts. The survey collected housing indicators in the areas of affordability, quality, finance, production, and subsidies, and regulatory indicators on the regulatory and institutional environment, for a total of 55 indicators and 224 variables. The results were published in 1992. The data comes from UNCHS and the World Bank. 1992. *The Housing Indicators Program Extensive Survey, Part II: Indicator Modules and Worksheets* (rev. March 1992). Also see Angel (2000) for data tables and interpretation of data.

Organisation for Economic Co-operation and Development (OECD) Data. This is a source of data for researchers and policy makers working on economic and policy issues covering twenty-nine member countries mainly in Europe *(www.oecd.org)*. Data on trends in international migration is published by OECD's SOPEMI (Systeme d'Observation Permanente sur les Migrations).

UN Millennium Indicators Data. The United Nations Secretariat and the specialized agencies of the UN system, as well as representatives of IMF, the World Bank, and OECD have defined a set of time-bound and measurable goals and targets for combating poverty, hunger, disease, illiteracy, environmental degradation, and discrimination against women. A framework of eight goals, eighteen targets, and forty-eight indicators was adopted. Data to track progress in meeting two of the goals in over two hundred countries are: equality indicators and sustainability indicators. United Nations Department of Economic and Social Affairs, Statistics Division, *millenniumindicators.un.org*

Equality Indicators. The third goal of the UN Millennium Declaration is to promote gender equality and empower women. The target to achieve this goal is to eliminate gender disparity in primary and secondary education, preferably by 2005, and in all levels of education no later than 2015. The UN has developed the following indicators to measure progress toward achievement of this goal:

- Ratio of girls to boys in primary, secondary, and tertiary education
- Ratio of literate women to men (ages 15 to 24)
- Share of women in wage employment in the nonagricultural sector
- Proportion of seats held by women in national parliament

Sustainability Indicators. The seventh goal of the UN Millennium Declaration is to ensure environmental sustainability. The target to achieve this goal is to integrate the principles of sustainable development into country policies and programs and reverse the loss of environmental resources. The UN has developed the following indicators to measure progress toward achievement of this goal:

- Proportion of land area covered by forest
- Ratio of area protected to maintain biological diversity to surface area
- Energy use (kg oil equivalent) per $1 Gross Domestic Product Purchasing Power Parity (GDP PPP)
- Carbon dioxide emissions (per capita)
- Proportion of population using solid fuels

Table 2.1   Main sources of international data on human settlements.

list of data sources for urban planners in Dandekar's edited volume *The Planner's Use of Information* (2003).

The discussion of spatial data will focus on a range of high-quality urban data including U.S. and international census data. These datasets were spatialized as part of a three-year National Science Foundation funded project started in 2003 at San Francisco State University titled, "Space, Culture, and Urban Policy: Integrating GIS into Research Methods Courses." These include the Asian Development Bank's *Cities Data Book* (Westfall and de Villa 2001), UN-HABITAT's Global Urban Indicators data (United Nations Centre for Human Settlements 1998), and the United Nations Centre for Human Settlements and World Bank's Housing Indicators data (1992). The data displayed in much of the maps in this book comes from these datasets *(table 2.1)*. The process of spatialization involved joining data tables with vector data (e.g., points and polygons) using ArcGIS software (as demonstrated in exercise 2).

Data for any analysis comes from two main sources: primary or secondary. Secondary data is information collected by an entity other than the researcher and often for other purposes. While the data gathered for other purposes often constrains researchers' selection of variables and geographies for analysis, it offers tremendous cost savings and convenience; therefore, researchers always start their investigation to see whether the data they seek has already been gathered by someone else. If the research project requires data that no one else has gathered, then the researcher has to carry out primary data collection activities.

U.S. population and housing data sources

The United States Decennial Census of Population and Housing. Census 2000 is the latest census, providing information about 115.9 million housing units and 281.4 million people across the United States. Summary File 1 (SF 1) and Summary File 3 (SF 3) are the most frequently used census datasets. The following tables show census data downloaded (July 2003) and analyzed for four U.S. MSAs (discussed in chapters 5 and 6).

Summary File 1: Demographics

Variable	Variable Name	# of Subvariables	Subvariables Extracted
P1	Total Population	1	1
P7	Race	8	8
P8	Hispanic or Latino by Race	17	17
P15	Households	1	1
P17	Average Household Size	1	1
P33	Average Family Size	1	1

Summary File 1: Housing

Variable	Variable Name	# of Subvariables	Subvariables Extracted
H3	Occupancy Status	3	3
H4	Tenure	3	3

Summary File 3: Demographics

Variable	Variable Name	# of Subvariables	Subvariables Extracted
P3	Total Population (100 Percent Count)	1	1
P21	Place of Birth by Citizenship Status	15	3
PCT19	Place of Birth for the Foreign-Born Population	126	6

Summary File 3: Immigration

Variable	Variable Name	# of Subvariables	Subvariables Extracted
P20	Household Language by Linguistic Isolation	14	7
P22	Year of Entry for the Foreign-Born Population	9	2
P24	Residence in 1995 for the Population 5 Years and Over—State and County Level	18	2

Summary File 3: Housing			
Variable	Variable Name	# of Subvariables	Subvariables Extracted
H7	Tenure	3	3
H20	Tenure by Occupants per Room	13	3
H50	Kitchen Facilities	3	3
H54	Contract Rent	24	24
H69	Gross Rent as a Percentage of Household Income in 1999	11	2
H76	Median Value (Dollars) for Specified Owner-Occupied Housing Units	1	1
H85	Median Value (Dollars) for all Owner-Occupied Housing Units	1	1
Summary File 3: Income			
Variable	Variable Name	# of Subvariables	Subvariables Extracted
P52	Household Income in 1999	17	17
P53	Median Household Income in 1999 (Dollars)	1	1
P76	Family Income in 1999	17	17
P77	Median Family Income in 1999 (Dollars)	1	1
P90	Poverty Status in 1999 of Families by Family Type by Presence of Related Children Under 18 Years by Age of Related Children	41	3
P92	Poverty Status in 1999 of Households by Household Type by Age of Householder	59	3

Table 2.2   Main sources of U.S. data on population and housing.

Standard survey research methods, as summarized by Nishikawa (2003), can be used to gather primary data specifically designed to answer the research questions at hand for which secondary data is not readily available.

Secondary data sources

Census data is by far the most widely used source of secondary data for urban planners and policy analysts. The U.S. Census Bureau is the lead federal agency in charge of collecting data on the U.S. population. The massive data collection effort by the U.S. Census Bureau is mandated by the U.S. Constitution, Article 1, Section 2. An accurate head count of the population is required for apportioning the 435 seats in the House of Representatives to the fifty states and to achieve representative democracy. The Census Bureau's three main data collection efforts produce extremely valuable data for urban planners and policy makers. The decennial census of population and housing collects detailed information on population and housing every ten years *(table 2.2)*. The American Community Survey (ACS) collects population and housing data on selected communities every three to five years. ACS data is available from 1996 and for an increasing number of communities. The ACS first obtained complete coverage of the United States in 2005. The Economic Census collects data on business establishments every five years. Altogether these three major data collection efforts result in the most comprehensive sources of data on people and their communities in the United States (Myers 1992; Peters and MacDonald 2004).

In 1990, the U.S. Census Bureau developed and introduced TIGER boundary data files to support its mapping needs. These files can be joined with census data on population and housing for spatial analysis. TIGER, which stands for Topologically Integrated Geographic Encoding and Referencing, is a digital database of geographic features, such as lines (e.g., roads) and polygons (e.g., census tracts). TIGER files are commonly used to map census data on population and housing, and are available for all fifty states, the District of Columbia, and Puerto Rico. One can download TIGER files free of charge directly from the U.S. Census Bureau Web site *(www.census.gov)* or from a third party such as ESRI *(www.esri.com/data)*.

Public Use Microdata Sample (PUMS) data files are used by social scientists interested in analyzing household level data. PUMS data files contain a sample of individual housing unit and person records from the census, along with sample weights. The U.S. Census Bureau releases this data for 1 percent and 5 percent samples of the households, and organizes the data geographically in Public Use Microdata Areas (PUMAs) for 5 percent sample data and Super PUMAs for 1 percent sample data. PUMAs have a minimum population size of 100,000; super-PUMAs have a minimum population size of 400,000. PUMAs fit within super-PUMAs. California, for example, has 62 super-PUMAs and 235 PUMAs. Chapter 1 of this book included a map of PUMAs in the San Francisco Bay region. Microdata files are also available from the ACS. This data provides the greatest possible detail while ensuring confidentiality, and is available free of charge from the U.S. Census Bureau *(www.census.gov/main/www/pums.html)*. American Community Survey PUMS data sample sizes are much smaller when compared to the decennial PUMS data.

Decennial censuses are important data-collection efforts in other countries as well, but the extent of data collection and reporting quality varies considerably across countries. Nonetheless, national census information on population and housing is an excellent secondary data source for urban planners worldwide. With census information on population and housing, simple indicators can be constructed to track the performance of land

and housing markets over time. When available, simple calculations can be undertaken from published tables, such as calculating simple percentage changes over time, comparing ratios over time, and computing percentiles, quintiles, and deciles. National publications based on the decennial census are especially useful for describing population and housing trends in small areas (at the census-tract or enumeration-district level) except in very rapidly changing cities where decennial census information may quickly become outdated. Small-area population and employment forecasting models developed and used by different government agencies and private sector consulting firms in the United States focus on providing data for the years between decennial censuses for small areas.

Data for cross-national analysis is available on a limited basis *(table 2.1)*. In the developing world data is gathered, analyzed, and reported by public agencies in a disjointed fashion and rarely made available on the Internet, making urban research informed by analysis of data much more difficult when compared to the United States. There are, however, several high-quality international data sources. Among these, a good source of high-quality, cross-national secondary data is the World Bank, which collects data on an annual basis and publishes it in its annual World Development Reports and atlases. Much of this data tracks economic and social conditions at the macro (i.e., country) level.

Another good source of cross-national secondary data for researchers working on economic and policy issues is the Organisation for Economic Cooperation and Development (OECD) covering twenty-nine member countries mostly in Europe *(www.oecd.org)*. Data on trends in international migration is published by OECD's SOPEMI *(Systeme d'Observation Permanente des Migrations)*. Other data collection efforts include Finland's Ministry of the Environment, Housing, and Building Department, which has compiled Housing Statistics in the European Union in 2001. Data for the publication comes from national ministries responsible for housing in the European Union member states, the European Mortgage Federation (EMF), and Eurostat. Housing Ministry of Belgium and Denmark's Ministry of Housing and Urban Affairs are leading the publication of 2002 and 2003–2004 issues, respectively, for the benefit of all European Union member states.

A more specialized cross-national dataset has been collected under the auspices of the Housing Indicators Program of the United Nations Centre for Human Settlements and the World Bank (UNCHS and World Bank 1992), which identified close to forty simple indicators to gauge the performance of the housing market. These are especially useful for cross-national comparisons in the world, and cross-regional comparisons. A key housing affordability indicator—house-price-to-income ratio—was defined as the ratio of median house price to median household income. A high value for this indicator (greater than 3) indicates that housing is too expensive for the majority of households. Map 2.1 shows house-price-to-income ratios for European cities for which data has been gathered from the Housing Indicators dataset. The global median value for the house-price-to-income ratio

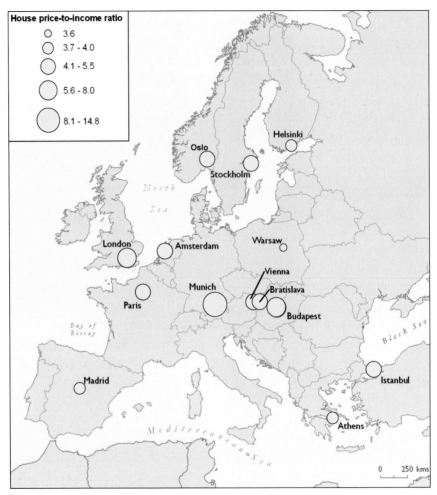

Map 2.1   House-price-to-income ratio in Europe, 1993.

Data sources: Housing Indicators Program data. Joint program of the United Nations Centre for Human Settlements and the World Bank, 1993.

in 1990 was 4.2, which indicates that median-income urban families paid a little over four times their annual household income for purchasing a median-priced house. Cities in the Middle East and North Africa region, and Eastern Europe reported higher than median values (6.4 and 7.0, respectively) (Angel 2000, 235). China reported 14.8 for this indicator. Indicators like the house-price-to-income ratio are important instruments of policy because they enable the monitoring of housing market and affordability conditions across countries and over time. The land development multiplier is another useful indicator collected by the Housing Indicators Program that measures the premium for providing infrastructure and converting raw land to residential use on the urban fringe. It is defined as the ratio of the

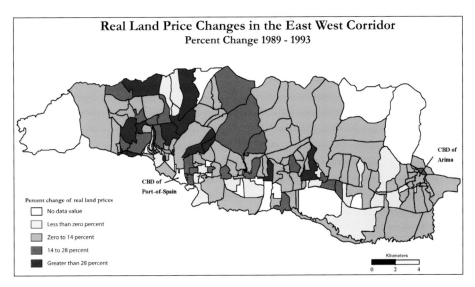

Map 2.2   Inflation-adjusted land price changes in the east-west corridor of western Trinidad, 1993.

Data source: Ayse Pamuk, 1993.

median land price of raw, undeveloped land in an area currently being developed. A high value for this indicator would suggest the presence of land supply restrictions (high regulatory constraints) (Pamuk 1994).

Primary data sources

When secondary data sources give inadequate answers, primary data should be collected. First-hand information on land and housing markets in developing countries can be gathered by land-price surveys (Dowall 1995), household surveys, aerial photography interpretation, and interviews with developers. Map 2.2 shows land-price data gathered through interviews with developers in Trinidad in 1993 (Pamuk and Dowall 1998). It shows real (inflation-adjusted) price changes between 1989 and 1993 in the major urban areas of Trinidad. Port-of-Spain and Arima are the two major cities in this urban region along the Caribbean Sea shoreline. Much of the steep price changes (more than 28 percent) during the study period have occurred in informal housing settlements occupied by households who can not afford prices in formal housing markets *(figures 1.8, 1.9, and 1.10).*

When primary data is unavailable, researchers often carry out special purpose surveys that are limited in scope. Urban planners frequently use survey methods to gather data for a small geographic area (e.g., neighborhood) or a specific subject matter (Nishikawa 2003). In Trinidad and Tobago, for example, a household survey I designed and implemented with the assistance of the national Central Statistical Office (CSO) in 1993 gathered information on household characteristics, housing conditions, access to land, housing construction and investment, housing finance, community participation, and rental housing. The information was important to understanding housing consumption patterns and different "paths to housing" used by households, which was otherwise unavailable through secondary information sources (Pamuk 1994).

Standardized data collection efforts

To reduce costs associated with spatializing data and to facilitate wider access to nonconfidential spatial data, a number of standardization efforts have been underway in the United States led by an Office of Management and Budget directive (OMB Circular A-119) and under the direction of the Federal Geographic Data Committee (FGDC). Standardization efforts of spatial data involve developing protocols for recording metadata—documentation about the spatial data, including map projection, sources of data, and the definition of variables. The excellent documentation system of the U.S. Census Bureau for census data, for example, facilitates easy use of the data and enables the replication of analyses by other researchers. The ability of other researchers to replicate the analysis for the same or different geographic areas is at the heart of social science research. Advances in social science knowledge over time is the result of careful incremental analysis of data that can be replicated using widely accepted research methods among scholars working in the same field. For these reasons, uniform data over time is very valuable for social scientists. Even when high-quality spatial data is available, there may be reluctance to use such data in certain disciplines where spatial analysis is not yet a standard method of analysis. Introduction of new analytical methods such as spatial analysis with GIS in traditionally nonspatial social science disciplines like economics and sociology to answer research questions is a relatively new phenomenon, as surveyed in *Spatially Integrated Social Science* by Goodchild and Janelle (2004).

National spatial data standardization efforts in other countries are loosely organized under the umbrella of the Global Spatial Data Infrastructure Network since their first meeting in 1996. Because of primarily cost-driven implementation challenges, a worldwide agreement and adoption of international spatial data standards can best be described as in infancy. Cultural differences may further slow the development and adoption of worldwide technology standards in building a global spatial data infrastructure. Not surprisingly, international organizations like the United Nations and the World Bank have particularly been interested in the development of international standards that would facilitate cross-national comparative analysis and monitoring of global indicators. These efforts, however, do not explicitly involve indicators measured by spatial data.

Access to high-quality spatial data (any type of data for that matter) in developing countries is very rudimentary. At present, limited efforts by international lending and aid agencies are insufficient for researchers and policymakers to carry out sophisticated analyses. A recent study documenting the state of the art in this area was funded by the University Consortium of Geographic Information Science (UCGIS) and U. S. Department of Housing and Urban Development (HUD). It found limited urban data in several developing countries included in the study (e.g., South Africa, Bostwana, and Kathmandu) (Hopkins et al. February 2002; *www.cobblestoneconcepts.com/ucgis2hud/finalHUDRptcontext.htm*).

The data collection and standardization efforts of international agencies on a global scale have been instrumental in advancing our comparative understanding of human settlement conditions around the world. Much of these efforts were showcased at the HABITAT II conference—the most recent international conference on human settlements, convened by the UN in Istanbul, Turkey (June 3–14, 1996). At this conference, governments formally adopted a range of global principles to monitor and solve human settlement problems in their countries. HABITAT II was preceded by a series of HABITAT-related activities since the first HABITAT conference in Vancouver, British Columbia (June 1976—HABITAT I). Of particular importance is the Urban Management Program—an interagency undertaking between the United Nations Development Programme (UNDP), United Nations Centre for Human Settlements (UNCHS), and the World Bank. Other milestones between 1976 and 1996 include the Global Shelter Strategy (United Nations Centre for Human Settlements 1988) and the Rio Declaration (United Nations 1992).

In essence, the HABITAT II conference marked the culmination of collaborative efforts worldwide over two decades to advance two principle goals: (1) shelter for all; and (2) sustainable human settlement development in an increasingly urban world. To ensure input from primary stakeholders throughout the world, the UN asked governments to prepare official national reports describing shelter and human settlements conditions, and policies in place for improvements. In the United States, the national report was prepared under the leadership of HUD, the State Department, and the U.S. Agency for International Development (USAID). To engage communities in the debate, a U.S. Network for HABITAT II, a nongovernmental organization (NGO), organized town meetings across the United States and brought core HABITAT II themes—civic engagement, sustainability, and equity—to local communities. Official meetings at the international level involved drafting and negotiating the contents of the principal HABITAT II document—the Global Plan of Action (also known as the HABITAT Agenda). In a second document produced at the conference—the Istanbul Declaration on Human Settlements—governments agreed to address lack of basic infrastructure and services, unsustainable population changes, and increased vulnerability to disasters among other priorities. The key innovations of the HABITAT II conference were (1) the incorporation of views from civil society institutions into the official HABITAT Agenda through the "partners" forum; (2) the emphasis on the role of local government agencies and NGOs in implementation; and (3) support of global partnerships and networks in finding solutions to human settlements problems.

The major initiatives for developing international urban indicators have followed three main conceptual schools. The first approach—the policy-based approach—has its root in the social indicators movement of the 1960s (Innes 1990) and aims to track key housing market performance indicators. This approach has been used by the World Bank/UNCHS Housing Indicators Program and the Global Urban Observatory of the United Nations. The United Nation's Millennium Indicators Program, for example, includes indicators to help track progress in reducing the number of people who live on less than one dollar a day worldwide. A framework for eight goals, eighteen targets, and forty-eight indicators was adopted *(table 2.1)*. One of the goals is to promote gender equality and empower women. The UN has developed four indicators to measure progress toward the achievement of this goal: (1) ratio of girls to boys in primary, secondary, and tertiary education; (2) ratio of

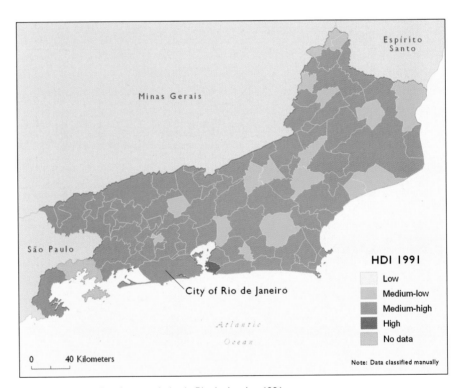

Map 2.3   Human Development Index in Rio de Janeiro, 1991.

Data sources: Instituto Brasileiro de Geografia e Estatística (IBGE)—Brazilian Census Bureau; Instituto de Pesquisa Economica Aplicada (IPEA), www.ipea.gov.br; United Nations Development Program (UNDP).

literate women to men (ages 15 to 24); (3) share of women in wage employment in the nonagricultural sector; and (4) proportion of seats held by women in national parliament. The data for over two hundred countries comes from the United Nations Department of Economic and Social Affairs, Statistics Division *(www.millenniumindicators.un.org)*.

The second approach—the thematic/index approach—identifies indicators to capture progress on broad themes rather than specific policy objectives. The United Nations Development Programme (UNDP) uses this approach. Themes such as livability, sustainability, or good governance are not directly observable, but involve aspects that can be measured by multiple indicators. A widely used example of the index approach is the UNDP's Human Development Index (HDI). As mentioned in chapter 1 of this book, the United Nations is in charge of constructing the HDI[1] to rank countries. The rankings are published in Human Development Reports (United Nations Development Programme 2003; *hdr.undp.org/hd*). The HDI ranges from zero to one. With a value of 0.77 in 2000, Brazil's human development is classified as medium. Maps 2.3 and 2.4 show HDI within the state

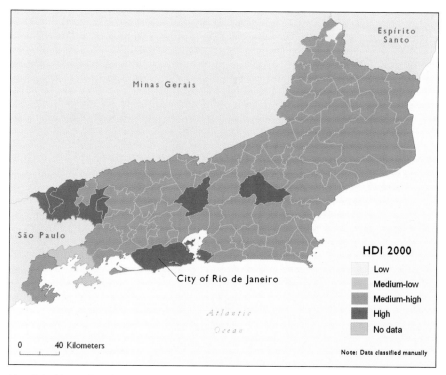

Map 2.4   Human Development Index in Rio de Janeiro, 2000.

Data sources: Instituto Brasileiro de Geografia e Estatistica (IBGE)—Brazilian Census Bureau; Instituto de Pesquisa Economica Aplicada (IPEA), www.ipea.gov.br; United Nations Development Program (UNDP).

of Rio de Janeiro in 1991 and 2000. In both 1991 and 2000, almost all of the municipalities are in the medium range, and the number of municipalities classified as having attained a high level of human development has increased between 1991 and 2000 *(maps 2.3 and 2.4)*. Not surprisingly, as a port city with global significance, Rio de Janeiro has attained high human development (HDI value of 0.84) as measured by this indicator. In 2000, none of the municipalities in the state of Rio de Janeiro had an HDI value below 0.5—a measure of low human development by worldwide standards.

The third approach—the systems approach—was originally developed by the Organisation for Economic Cooperation and Development (OECD), and attempts to make indicators reflect cause-and-effect relationships between various actors. Though this approach attempts to capture the complexity, it lacks the goals-oriented focus found in the other approaches (Newton 2001).

Measuring the magnitude of informal housing settlements in the developing world has attracted considerable attention from policy makers. As mentioned in the introduction of this book, informal housing settlements are widespread in the developing world, especially in "megacities" like Bombay, São Paulo, Shanghai, Mexico City, and Rio de Janeiro. Residents of informal housing settlements (called *favelados* in Rio de Janeiro's favelas, for example) do not have legal title to the land they occupy, and therefore are considered to live in unauthorized status, vulnerable to evictions or demolitions at any time. In measuring land tenure status, United Nations HABITAT's Global Urban Observatory and the Asian Development Bank (ADB) include data on land tenure types like private rental, social housing, and rent-free tenure. Nonetheless, the fact that only four out of the seventeen cities included in the ADB's *Cities Data Book* (Westfall and de Villa 2001) could provide statistics for every tenure category, points to the complexity of land tenure and how it often eludes cross-national generalizations. Moreover, as Flood (1997) notes, global indicators are often not used as developing nations resist introduction of "top-down" indicators by international lending and aid agencies. In the absence of standardized data, comparative analysis of informal housing settlement conditions worldwide is difficult. Recently UN-HABITAT developed a method to estimate unauthorized housing settlements. The UN-HABITAT Slum Estimates Data is based on data produced by the Human Settlements Statistics Questionnaire. The questionnaire, most recently administered in 1999, gathered data on population, housing, and social and economic conditions for 315 cities in 91 countries. The data is available from the UN-HABITAT office in Nairobi, Kenya *(www.unchs.org/ programmes/guo/guo_indicators.asp)*.

In addition, the World Bank has launched a major initiative to create "Cities without Slums" *(www.citiesalliance.org/citiesalliancehomepage.nsf)*.

	Raster	Vector
Primary	digital satellite remote sensing images digital aerial photographs	GPS measurements survey measurements
Secondary	scanned maps or photographs digital elevation models from topographic map contours	topographic maps toponymy (place name) databases

Table 2.3   Classification of spatial data for data collection purposes.

Source: Adapted from Paul A. Longley, Michael F. Goodchild, David J. Maguire, and David W. Rhind. *Geographic Information Systems and Science,* 2nd ed. (Chichester, West Sussex, England: John Wiley and Sons, 2005). © John Wiley and Sons Ltd. Reproduced with permission.

Sources of spatial data

As discussed in chapter 1 of this book, GIS analysis uses spatial data in vector or raster formats, which can originate from diverse sources *(table 2.3).* Primary spatial data is collected for a particular purpose and use in GIS. The most popular form of primary spatial data capture is remote sensing, which is gathered without physical contact with the subject being studied. Information is based on the "measurements of the amount of electromagnetic radiation reflected, emitted, or scattered from objects" (Longley et al. 2005, 202). Resolution (spatial, spectral, and temporal) is a key characteristic of data captured by remote sensing technology. Spatial resolution is measured by pixel size. Satellite remote sensing devices capture data in the range of one meter to one kilometer. Primary raster data can be collected by SPOT (Satellite Probatoire d'Observation de la Terre) and IKONOS Earth satellite images. Primary vector data measurements can be collected through a survey instrument (Longley et al. 2005, 200–01). Aerial photographs are equally important mechanisms used to capture primary spatial data, which can later be converted into raster format. The cameras used for aerial photography usually cover a range from 0.1 meter to 5 meters. Data captured by remote sensing and aerial photographs are used to build digital elevation models. Chapter 1 included an elevation model for San Francisco *(figure 1.4 and map 1.16 in chapter 1).* Another method of primary data capture is by global positioning systems (GPS), intensively used by private sector firms in the United States that use spatial information for routine business transactions like mail and package delivery.

   Secondary data sources are those gathered for another purpose, but can be used in GIS after appropriate conversions. These include raster aerial photographs of urban areas that can be scanned and converted into vector data format for analysis. In developing countries, aerial photographs are used to monitor any unauthorized house construction activity on ecologically sensitive lands like wetlands, floodplains, and hillsides prone to erosion. Favelas in Brazil are often built in such locations, increasing their vulnerability to natural disasters. The growth of new settlements identified by aerial photography over time can be translated onto paper maps and incorporated into land-use planning. Another important method of secondary

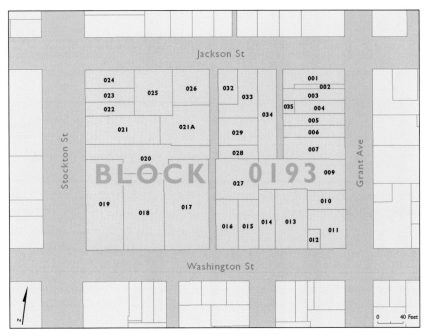

Map 2.5   San Francisco parcel map.

spatial data capture is scanning. Scanned maps are frequently used in GIS analysis. These maps are converted into vector format for analysis. Maps can also be digitized directly from hard copy and analyzed as vector data. Map 2.2, showing land price changes in the port city of Port-of-Spain—the capital city of the twin island country of Trinidad and Tobago—was produced by digitizing a paper map placed on a digitizing tablet.

Another crucial information system for urban planners and city managers is the cadastre. The cadastre is the map of landownership in an area maintained for the purpose of taxation and creating a public record of ownership (Longley et al. 2005, 114). Increasingly, municipalities across the United States are providing searchable online databases where anyone with access to the Internet can look up ownership information, assessed value of properties, and square footage information. Map 2.5 shows a parcel map for a section of San Francisco with individual parcel identification numbers. One can search a parcel number or an address on the San Francisco tax assessor's Web site *(gispubweb.sfgov.org/website/ sfparcel/index.htm)* and obtain landownership information.

Data quality

Rapid advances in information technology, increased access to the Internet, and availability of powerful computers at affordable prices have resulted in easier access to secondary data by a wide range of population groups. Over the past decade, increasing access to data by anyone with an Internet connection has revolutionized analyses and interpretations of data and has contributed to the increased access of data (Sawicki and Craig 1996). The U.S. Census Bureau, for example, has created a user-friendly American FactFinder system on the Internet that makes census data downloading by anyone with an Internet connection possible.

Ironically, the availability of vast amounts of data on the Internet, coupled with the ease of accessing online data sources, increasingly requires sophistication in judging the reliability and quality of data. Data posted on Web sites by government agencies (e.g., U.S. Census Bureau), think tanks (e.g., Urban Institute, Brookings Institution), and international organizations (e.g., UN-HABITAT, the World Bank) come with extensive documentation of data collection methods and a discussion of any limitations of the data. Data without adequate documentation should be viewed as highly suspect and handled with caution.

Policy significance of data and types of analysis with spatial data

The data that government agencies collect has very specific purposes. For example, data on the number of households living under the federal poverty threshold for cities is required in order to justify the flow of federal assistance dollars to qualified jurisdictions. Similarly, household income data collected by the U.S. Census Bureau is used to define eligibility criteria for public assistance. For example, public housing assistance is available based on the following eligibility definitions that compare prospective beneficiary household's income to area median household income thresholds: extremely low-income households (30 percent of area median household income and below), very low-income households (30–50 percent), and low-income (50–80 percent). To implement the Section 8 voucher program, HUD publishes fair market rents (FMR) for all localities in the United States, which are used to determine the amount of gap the government needs to cover to assist eligible households.

Policy relevant data (e.g., households living in poverty) gathered by government agencies for the implementation of programs (e.g., Temporary Assistance for Needy Families or TANF) is not always explicitly concerned with recording spatial information. Basic spatial information automatically collected by government agencies like the home address of beneficiaries, however, can be easily incorporated into spatial analysis. To protect the confidentiality of individuals, administrative data can only be released at aggregate geographic levels (e.g., ZIP Code) and for purposes permitted by law. For example, researchers can have access to microdata files from HUD for research on housing and community development policy-related questions. No unique identifiers (e.g., name, Social Security number, date of birth, or address is included). Files are part of a Privacy Act system, and their use is governed by a 1997 Federal Register Notice on democratizing data (Gray and Haley 2003). HUD also provides public housing project geocodes to facilitate mapping *(www.huduser. org/datasets/assthsg/statedata98/index.html)*.

Government agencies can carry out detailed spatial analysis with in-house data they routinely collect in the course of administering programs. Such analysis is, however, seldom done unless agencies gain access to external technical expertise (e.g., universities). A good example is the analysis carried out by the San Francisco Head Start Program, under the auspices of San Francisco State University. This program uses home address data collected for program implementation purposes and also used in an in-house analysis to understand the distances children traveled to get to existing Head Start centers. Such analysis requires that the data collected (e.g., street address of centers) can be georeferenced (discussed in chapter 3). Using GIS, one can geographically relate nonspatial data collected for administrative purposes and stored in a spreadsheet (e.g., Head Start center addresses) with a street map. This process of spatializing data can be time consuming and expensive, but once in place offers tremendous benefits over the long run.

Analysis of spatial data can involve cross-sectional data (e.g., Asian population in San Francisco in 2000) or temporal data (e.g., change in Asian population between 1990 and 2000). Urban planners routinely carry out analyses of census data over time to understand change of neighborhoods (Myers 1992; Peters and MacDonald 2004). Such analyses need

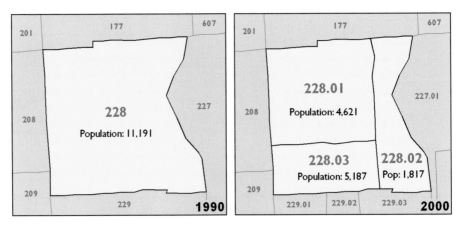

Figure 2.1   Census tract boundary changes, 1990–2000.

Data sources: U.S. Census Bureau, Census 1990 and 2000 TIGER/Line data down to the census tract level.

to take into account comparability of data over time due to any changes in census tract boundaries between the two years of analysis (e.g., 1990 and 2000). As certain census tracts gain population, the U.S. Census Bureau splits tracts to maintain an average population size of about 4,000 people. Figure 2.1 shows how census tract 228 in San Francisco's Mission District in 1990 was split into three tracts in 2000.

Analysis of change can involve absolute or percentage values. Using 1990 census tract boundaries, map 2.6 shows Asian population change (absolute values) between 1990 and 2000. It shows that western and southern portions of San Francisco have gained more than seven hundred households per census tract between 1990 and 2000. Map 2.7 shows the percentage change of Asian population during the same period. Urban planners frequently use these types of maps to understand change in neighborhoods between decennial censuses, and incorporate results into activities concerned with community planning.

As discussed in this chapter, spatial data—a crucial component of spatial analysis using GIS—comes from a variety of sources. Data standardization efforts led by government

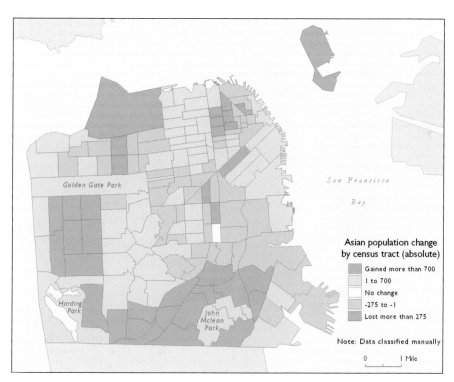

Map 2.6   Asian population change (absolute) by census tract, 1990–2000.

Data sources: U.S. Census Bureau, Census 1990 Summary Tape File 1 (STF 1), Census 2000 Summary File 1 (SF1), Asian population variable (P007005); Census 1990 TIGER/Line data down to the census tract level.

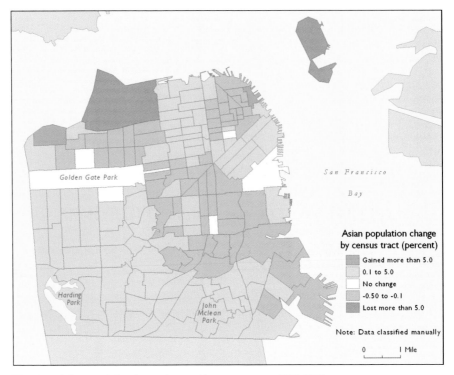

Map 2.7 Asian population change (percent) by census tract, 1990–2000.

Data sources: U.S. Census Bureau, Census 1990 Summary Tape File 1 (STF 1), Census 2000 Summary File 1 (SF1), Asian population variable (P007005); Census 1990 TIGER/Line data down to the census tract level.

agencies in the United States and the work of international development agencies concerned with monitoring indicators (e.g., human development) worldwide has gained new momentum. Advances in GIS software increasingly make it easier to carry out analysis with spatial data by novice and advanced urban planners and policy analysts alike. Spatial analysis using GIS has now emerged as a powerful analytical tool in a wide range of settings from international agencies to local government planning departments. The next chapter will discuss types of GIS applications most widely used in local government and regional planning agencies in a number of countries and settings.

Notes

1   For a description of the method used to construct the HDI for each country see *hdr.undp. org/reports/global/2003/pdf/hdr03_backmatter_2.pdf*.

Part **2**

Urban planning and policy applications with GIS

Chapter 3

Urban planning applications of GIS in local government

The use of computers in planning began during the 1960s with much optimism. Building large-scale metropolitan land-use and transportation models became possible with increased computing capacity. At the same time, the field of urban planning was strongly influenced by policy analysis with its intellectual origins in systems engineering, management science, and political and administrative sciences (Friedmann 1987).

In the 1970s the optimism faded when planning academics severely questioned the rational planning model and the use of large-scale urban models for public planning applications. Planners' enthusiasm for computer-based decision support systems, however, resumed in the 1980s with the development of microcomputers. The 1990s brought another wave of enthusiasm with the increased availability and accessibility of desktop computers and geographic information systems. This was also a period when the dominant view regarding the role of information technology in planning became much more positive. Information infrastructure came to be viewed as vital for social interaction and better communication to achieve common societal goals (Klosterman 2001).

GIS education has now become a standard component of urban planning curricula in all graduate programs offering master's degrees in city and regional planning *(www.acsp.org)* and many undergraduate programs offering urban studies degrees. It also has emerged in the curricula of public policy schools in the United States *(www.appam.org)*. GIS use and applications in urban planning and public policy outside of academia is wide-ranging in scope and a growing area.

Indeed, a wide range of community planning activities carried out by local governments, social service delivery agencies, community-based nonprofit organizations, and advocacy groups can benefit from GIS analysis. In contrast to sophisticated computer modeling efforts of the 1960s that were carried out using mainframe computers and complex computer programming languages, the new wave of GIS applications are far more accessible to non-GIS specialists. Moreover, what makes GIS effective in solving urban planning and public policy problems has a lot to do with the capability of planners and policy analysts (with appropriate training) to effectively blend GIS computer operations with subject-area knowledge. As GIS operations become easier to navigate by nonspecialist local government staff, time will be freed up to undertake advanced problem solving in community planning.

At present, several seemingly stubborn barriers impede wider use of GIS in local government agencies. These barriers include lack of resources in organizations and the limited planning functionality of standard GIS software (French and Wiggins 1990; Innes and Simpson 1993). Institutional inertia also plays a role in cases where new technology can face resistance from practitioners who might otherwise benefit from an increase in efficiency and effectiveness in doing their routine tasks with GIS. Such challenges have been widely discussed in the technology diffusion literature (Nedovic-Budic 2000).

This chapter provides an overview of fundamental GIS applications being used most frequently by practitioner planners and policy makers in local government and nonprofit settings, and illustrates how they are being deployed in solving community planning problems. GIS can be applied to many areas in government: housing, social service delivery, the geographic analysis of demographics, education, economic development, transportation and services routing, infrastructure, health, tax maps, law enforcement, land-use planning, parks and recreation, environmental monitoring, and emergency management (O'Looney 2000, 90-91; Greene 2000).

Efficiency and equity are two commonly used evaluative criteria to determine the extent to which GIS applications have resulted in success (O'Looney 2000, 92; Bardach 2005). The efficiency criterion considers cost-effectiveness of program implementation and is widely used in cost-benefit studies. GIS is particularly well suited to increasing efficiency in an area like law enforcement, a field where one can monitor incidences and types of crimes in small areas using GIS, thus enabling police patrols to be directed into areas with high crime rates. The use of GIS in a public emergency situation is another area where efficiency and quick action is necessary during post-disaster response. The rescue, relief, and clean-up activities after the September 11, 2001, terrorist attacks on the World Trade Center in New

York City, for example, benefited from GIS use (Clarke 2005), as did similar efforts after hurricanes devastated the U.S. Gulf Coast region in 2005 *(www.ucgis.org/katrina)*.

Ensuring equity in the delivery of social services is another important government goal that can benefit from GIS analysis (discussed further in the case of San Francisco's Head Start program in chapter 4). It is widely understood that the geography of opportunity is uneven in many cities, especially global cities like Rio de Janeiro and New York (Pamuk and Cavallieri 1998; Marcuse and van Kempen 2000; Briggs 2005). The close proximity of Rio de Janeiro's favelas to high-end housing developments, for example, presents a striking image of inequality in Brazil. Using maps one can visually communicate disparities in income and housing conditions powerfully. Such inequities are often hard to detect and communicate by analyses of data using tables alone. Geographic analysis of demographics is another application of GIS that advances the goal of equity. Such demographic analyses can increase public awareness of population diversity—information that can be used to better reach out to different demographic groups and facilitate citizen participation in public policy.

Classification of place into spatial units for analysis

A well-designed GIS analysis begins with the identification of appropriate units of analysis. Chapter 1 discussed different types of spatial units used in urban analysis. For example, the U.S. Census Bureau has divided cities into blocks, block groups, and census tracts for data collection purposes. The uniform method of creating geographic entities throughout the country enables analyses at different geographic scales that relate to one another. For example, one can compare median household income at the census tract level to figures at the county or state level (reference area) to obtain a comparative understanding.

Urban planners aggregate geographic entity boundaries (e.g., census block, block group, tract) as appropriate to create neighborhood boundaries for analysis and to develop area plans. Census geographic entity boundaries typically follow major roads and topographic features; so when planners create new zones using these entities, the end-result is a reasonably good proxy for the area mentally defined by local residents as their neighborhood. In fact, cognitive mapping studies (Lynch 1960) reveal areas of cities where residents attribute certain names, which can later be used by planners to define appropriate zones in GIS analysis to inform community planning.

Defining neighborhood boundaries accurately is crucial because much of the analysis of census data to support community planning activities uses this area definition. GIS can be used as a tool in participatory planning activities as it can provide spatial context, interactivity, and can serve as a vehicle to incorporate different viewpoints from the community into the analysis (Talen 2000). In the event planners and neighborhood residents disagree on the boundaries of the neighborhood, stakeholders can come up with their own aggregation of the data and analysis. Increased access to spatial data and census data (discussed in chapter 2) has led to empowerment of citizens concerned with public-sector actions in their neighborhoods. Armed with their own analyses of the same data, community-based groups now can challenge, if necessary, analyses produced by other entities. Parker and Pascual (2002) describe the gentrification battles in San Francisco's South of Market neighborhood in the 1990s and the role GIS played in helping communities advance their own arguments about changes in the neighborhood. GIS analysis was a vital tool in the "parcel politics" that played out in that period. Public participation GIS (PPGIS) is a growing field with a large number of similar examples of GIS use in community planning *(www. urisa.org/ppgis/ppgis.htm)*.

Many seasoned, community-based organizations with in-house GIS expertise routinely carry out analyses, reducing their complete reliance on the analyses produced by city planning departments, especially involving controversial project proposals. Community Outreach Partnership Centers (COPC) are also capable of producing demographic and housing analyses for neighborhood-based organizations. This activity meshes well with the community service learning philosophy many universities hold. However, university assistance to communities with mapping is sporadic except in the context of externally funded programs such as those led by the Office of University Partnerships (OUP) of the U.S. Department of Housing and Urban Development (Rubin 1998), and when supported by university resources during the post-grant period.

Different stakeholders concerned with the well-being of communities use various methods to geographically divide the city for analysis. For planning purposes, urban planners divide the city into planning subareas, large geographic areas that may or may not match zone boundaries and names familiar to local residents, as mentioned above. Social service providers, on the other hand, work with ZIP Code areas and rely on statistics collected and reported at this geographic level of detail. Elected officials pay attention to data at the voting district level. GIS provides great flexibility in creating zones and geographic areas appropriate for the type of analysis at hand. When working with GIS one can either use existing boundaries (e.g., census tract, ZIP Code) or create entirely new zones (e.g., immigrant clusters) for analysis (discussed in chapters 5 and 6, and demonstrated in exercise 5 and the self-directed project). Map 3.1 shows different spatial classifications of San Francisco.

Types of GIS applications

Two main categories of GIS applications in local government and nonprofit settings are noteworthy: (1) inventory applications; and (2) policy analysis applications. Inventory applications include locating property information such as ownership and tax assessments

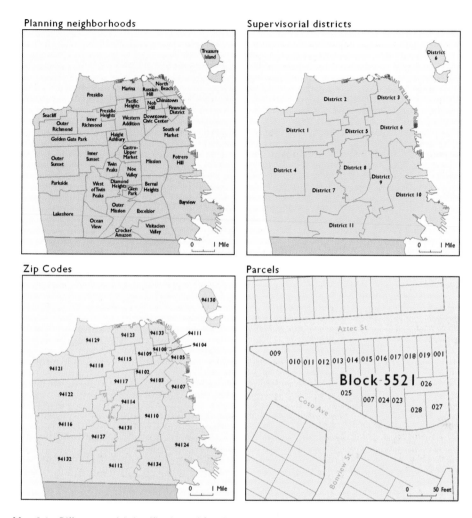

Map 3.1 Different spatial classifications of San Francisco.

by querying a GIS attribute table or by directly clicking on a map to access information about geographic features. Policy analysis applications include thematic mapping and proximity analysis. Management and policy-making applications include facility siting analysis, which may involve multilayer analysis. This chapter will further discuss these generic types of GIS applications most commonly used by practitioners with examples.

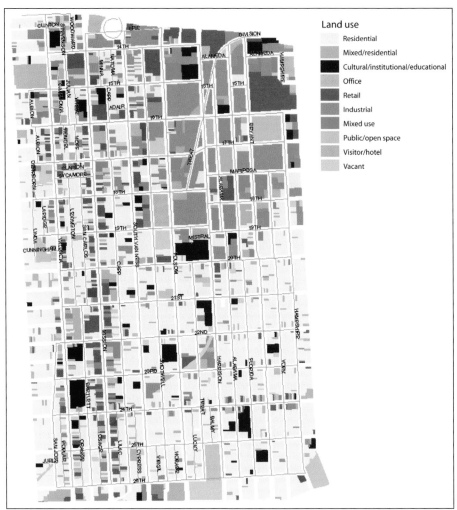

Map 3.2   Land-use map of San Francisco's Mission District.

Source: © San Francisco Planning Department, Citywide Policy and Analysis. SF Planning, Eastern Neighborhood Rezoning Team.

Inventory applications

As discussed in chapter 1, a GIS map connected to an attribute table offers the possibility of queries. Querying allows the computer user to interactively obtain information about geographic features displayed on the computer screen. The querying ability of a well-designed GIS can provide significant cost savings in answering citizen inquiries by social service agencies (O'Looney 2000, 15). Many local government agencies take advantage of this simple querying function of GIS and have developed inventory GIS databases such as land-records inventories, land-use inventories, housing inventories, and so on.

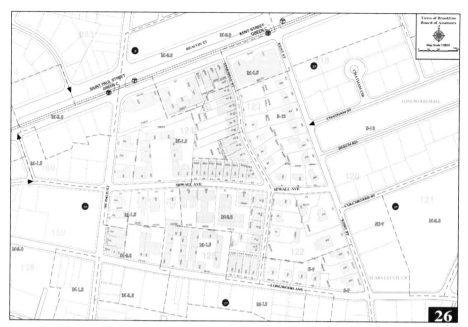

Map 3.3   Assessor's map of Brookline, Massachusetts.

Source: Geographic Information Systems Department, Town of Brookline, Massachusetts. © Town of Brookline, a municipal corporation located in Norfolk County, Massachusetts.

Map 3.2 shows the land-use map of the Mission District in San Francisco using standard land-use categories: residential, retail, industrial, public/open space, and so on. Each parcel of land has a land-use and a zoning designation, and any new development has to comply with these regulations in order to secure a building permit. Planning and building permit department staff can quickly query the GIS database to identify a specific parcel's designation.

Map 3.3 is another example of an inventory GIS application. It shows parcel data—a cadastre map—from the tax assessor's office of the city of Brookline, Massachusetts. As mentioned in chapter 2 of this book, a cadastre is the map of landownership and is used for taxation purposes. Tax assessors can quickly query the database to look up ownership and land value information.

Inventory GIS databases are particularly helpful in coordination with multijurisdictional levels of government. Agencies are increasingly creating protocols and standards to make data sharing across agencies possible and facilitate the delivery of information and services to the public on the Internet. The e-government literature documents widespread use of online methods of delivering government services to the public, including information services such as online tax assessment and landownership data provided by tax assessor offices around the country. State and local governments are increasingly becoming "cyberactive" (Stowers 1999).

Policy analysis applications

Many local government agencies and nonprofit organizations use GIS to carry out analyses to inform grant applications they submit to government agencies and foundations to fund city programs. Thematic mapping is widely used in these reports. Another widely used analytical application of GIS that informs policy making is georeferencing. Community-based organizations, in particular, use GIS to display the locations of facilities and resources in the community. Community asset mapping (Kretzman and McKnight 1994) is an important analytical application of GIS and valuable in documenting neighborhood resources (e.g., parks, schools, libraries). Once these facilities are georeferenced, additional analytical operations can be carried out, including buffering and proximity analysis (discussed subsequently).

Thematic mapping

As discussed in chapter 1, thematic mapping involves mapping of feature attribute characteristics (e.g., census variables like median household income). Choropleth (shaded area) maps are the most widely produced type of thematic maps by urban planners as part of preparing a range of reports for federal grant applications. One significant effort involves preparing a Consolidated Plan document to obtain four types of interrelated federal grants: emergency shelter grants, HOME[1] grants, Community Development Block Grants, and McKinney grants for assisting the homeless *(www.hud.gov/library/bookshelf18/archivedsum. cfm)*. Local government agencies include thematic maps of community demographics using census data in these reports. In addition, urban planners use thematic mapping to communicate with neighborhood residents more effectively in the context of community planning activities. Map images are particularly powerful in community planning *charettes*[2] where community input is sought for long-range land-use planning activities.

Previous chapters already featured a range of thematic maps showing locations of children under 5 years of age in poverty in San Francisco *(map 1.13)*, the foreign-born population in Paris *(map 1.4)*, and favela population concentrations in Rio de Janeiro *(map 1.11)*. Here, additional maps from governmental agencies are included. Maps 3.4, 3.5, and 3.6 show concentrations of immigrants from other European Union countries, Africa (except Maghreb), and Turkey, respectively, in the Paris metropolitan region from IAURIF (Institut d'Aménagement et d'Urbanisme de la Region d'Île-de-France). IAURIF is a planning agency with its origins in a 1960 central government initiative to develop a master plan for

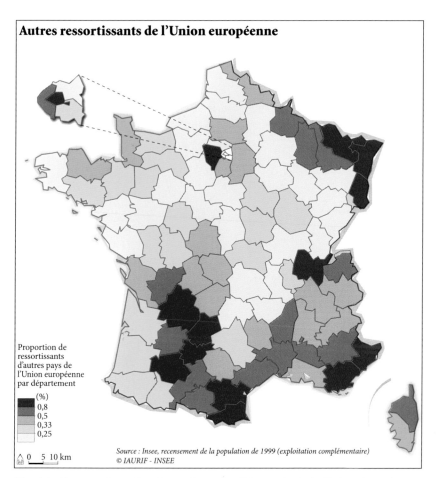

Map 3.4   Concentrations of immigrants from other EU countries in the Paris region and France, 1999.

Source: Atlas des Franciliens, tome 3, 2002 © IAURIF-INSEE.

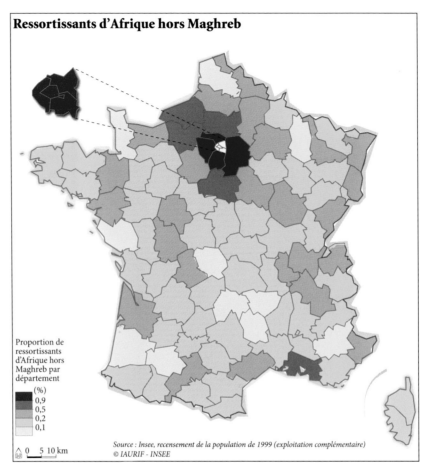

Map 3.5 Concentrations of immigrants from Africa (except those from Maghreb in North Africa) in the Paris region and France, 1999.

Source: Atlas des Franciliens, tome 3, 2002 © IAURIF-INSEE.

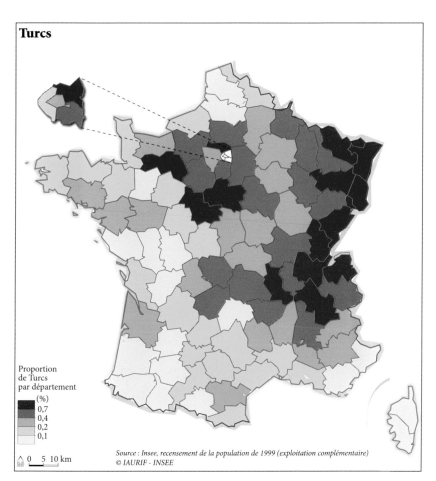

Turcs

Proportion
de Turcs
par département
(%)
0,7
0,4
0,2
0,1

0   5   10 km

Source : Insee, recensement de la population de 1999 (exploitation complémentaire)
© IAURIF - INSEE.

Map 3.6   Concentrations of immigrants from Turkey in the Paris region and France, 1999.

Source: Atlas des Franciliens, tome 3, 2002 © IAURIF-INSEE.

the Paris region. Since 1982, the agency works under the authority of the elected Île-de-France Regional Council. Its main goals include developing and recommending general and sector-based regional planning and development policies. A multidisciplinary team of experts provide research and analysis, including spatial analysis with GIS, to inform regional planning activities in the Île-de-France region. In the sequence of maps on pages 77–79, map 3.4 shows the heaviest concentrations of immigrants from other European countries mostly in the south and eastern areas of France, as indicated by the darker shadings on the map. Map 3.5 shows heavy concentrations of African immigrants (except those from Maghreb) in and around Paris, in the central-north area of the country. There is also a heavy concentration in the southeast (dark red). Map 3.6 shows heavy concentrations of Turkish immigrants in the eastern part of France, particularly, and in some central regions.

Maps 3.7, 3.8, and 3.9 show informal housing settlements in the municipality of Rio de Janeiro (with a 2000 population of about 12.5 million inhabitants) on GIS maps created by IPP (Instituto Municipal de Urbanismo Pereira Passos). IPP *(www.rio.rj.gov.br/ipp)* monitors favela development within municipal boundaries using GIS analysis and analyzes census data to inform the municipality's Favela-Bairro program[3] (Pamuk and Cavallieri 1998). Map 3.7 shows the population living in favelas in 2000 using census data. Map 3.8 shows the location of favela neighborhoods in 2004 overlaid with the topography of the city. Notice that some of the favelas are located on hillsides and terrain not suitable for development (as indicated by the dark red areas adjacent to or on the dark green, higher elevation areas). Favelas are settlements built on government land without building permits. Rocinha *(figures 1.5 and 1.6)* is located on the southeast corner of the municipality of Rio de Janeiro *(map 3.8).*

Map 3.9 shows another type of informal housing settlement common in Rio de Janeiro—illegal subdivisions *(loteamentos irregulars ou clandestinos).* This type of settlement differs from favelas in that the dwellers do not squat on land owned by others (the government in most cases) but rather buy a plot from the owner who has subdivided the land without government approvals. Under current laws in Brazil, residents in these settlements cannot obtain title to their lands. Notice that these neighborhoods are concentrated in the western part of the city (as indicated by the dark red clusters). The municipality's Favela-Bairro program involves only favelas, where residents are assisted in the process of obtaining titles to their land.

When interpreting choropleth maps (e.g., maps 3.4, 3.5, and 3.6 in this chapter), viewers must be mindful of the modifiable area unit problem (MAUP). This is a problem Openshaw (1984) discusses at great length and which has been noted by many others (DeMers 2005, 422; Longley et al. 2005, 148). The MAUP involves obtaining conflicting results from different area unit definitions. Mapmakers and researchers should pay attention to this problem and investigate whether the problem exists or not by undertaking simulations

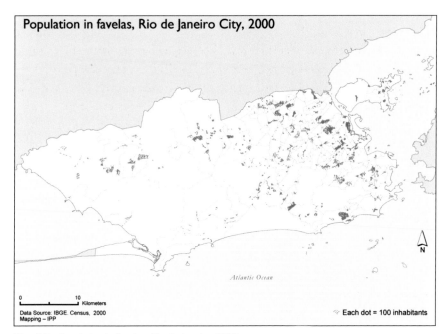

Map 3.7 Population in favelas, Rio de Janeiro, 2000.

Source: Instituto Pereira Passos (IPP) Rio de Janeiro.

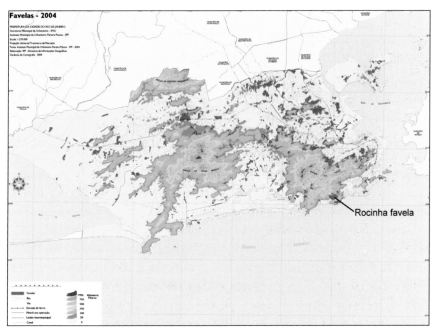

Map 3.8 Favelas of Rio de Janeiro, 2004.

Source: Instituto Pereira Passos (IPP) Rio de Janeiro.

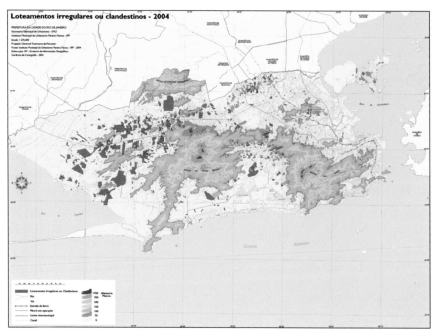

Map 3.9   Illegal subdivisions (loteamentos irregulares ou clandestinos), Rio de Janeiro, 2004.

Source: Instituto Pereira Passos (IPP) Rio de Janeiro.

using a large number of alternative zoning schemes. If the results show sensitivity to different zonal classifications, then the results can not be considered robust and reliable. The problem is particularly acute when working with spatial units like census tracts in the urban planning field. By design, census tracts each contain about 4,000 people, and the Census Bureau splits census tracts when they exceed that level, as shown in figure 2.1. This means that in sparsely populated unincorporated areas of counties the census tracts are large when compared to smaller inner-city census tracts. As a result of this spatial unit definition the U.S. Census Bureau has created for statistical purposes, large areas on choropleth maps may be colored to indicate incidences of a phenomenon that may not be as dominant as the map image conveys. The best strategy is to be familiar with the distribution of the underlying data and make a judgment regarding the most appropriate approach for mapping, which might include mapping absolute figures or percentages, or mapping normalized data by land area (e.g., population per square mile). The ultimate goal of the mapmaker should be to convey the data accurately and not create misinterpretations that might originate from the shape of the spatial unit of analysis.

Ecological fallacy is another problem that novice mapmakers and users may encounter. This is the problem of making disaggregate statements from aggregate data (DeMers 2005, 422; Longley et al. 2005, 156–48). For example, the U.S. Census Bureau data widely used and downloaded using the American FactFinder comes as aggregate data at the block, block group, census tract, etc., level. For a particular census tract, for example, we can obtain data on median household income. As discussed previously, the U.S. Census Bureau does not release household level data, so as to protect the confidentiality of respondents. By definition, median indicates that half of the households in that particular census tract have household income below the median and half above it. Suppose the median household income in San Francisco's census tract number 329 is $80,000. If the majority of the households in that particular census tract are born in China, one might jump to the conclusion that the China-born population in this particular census tract has a median household income of $80,000. This may or may not be true depending on the distribution of income in that particular census tract for all households. Without additional data (e.g., local ethnographic data), any inferences made from aggregate data to household level might result in the problem of ecological fallacy.

Great care needs to be given to interpretation of such data from maps, and results must be corroborated from other data sources before one can conclude that indeed the China-born population in census tract 329 has household income at the median. Working with PUMS data at the household level would fix this problem at first sight because it would enable one to make statements about income of the China-born population. However, as discussed earlier, the unit of analysis for PUMS data—PUMA—covers a very large geographic area *(map 1.2)*, which is not helpful for neighborhood-level analysis. While not using these exact terms (i.e., the modifiable area unit problem and ecological fallacy), Mark Monmonier discusses common pitfalls mapmakers and users can avoid in his popular and accessible book *How to Lie with Maps* (Monmonier 1996). Above all, as with any nonspatial analysis of policy-relevant data, one should take mapmakers' credibility and ethical integrity into account when relying on maps others have created.

To carry out proximity analysis (discussed below), the data first needs to be geocoded. Geographic features with known street addresses can be matched to known geographic locations on the surface of the earth; this is called the GIS geocoding function.

Geographic location is at the heart of spatial analysis with GIS. Different methods have been developed to specify the location of an element on the earth's surface. *Georeference*, *geolocate*, and *geocode* are words used to describe the act of assigning location information to items of interest. The most common method of locating an object starts by identifying the object's latitude and longitude. Map projection transforms a position on the earth's surface identified by latitude and longitude into a position in Cartesian coordinates (x,y). GIS enables the conversion between projections and coordinate systems to ensure an accurate two-dimensional representation of geographic features situated on earth. Global positioning systems (GPS) are particularly attractive because one can see the latitude and longitude or the universal transverse Mercator (UTM) coordinates of a particular location on earth directly on the device. UTM coordinates are in meters, allowing users to make accurate measurements for short distances with the use of a handheld GPS device.

Working with map projections can be tricky and should be handled with care. GIS software makes it easy to convert map projections, but one needs to make informed choices about appropriate map projections. Maps using simply latitude as *x* and longitude as *y* are known as unprojected projection, and present a distorted image of the earth. Common map projections include the Mercator projection and Lambert conformal conic projection, both of which preserve the property of local shape, which ensures that the outline of a small area like a state or part of a coastline are correct. These are called conformal projections (Clarke 2003, 41). Metropolitan area maps in this book have been produced using a Lambert conformal conic projection, making it possible to accurately measure distance

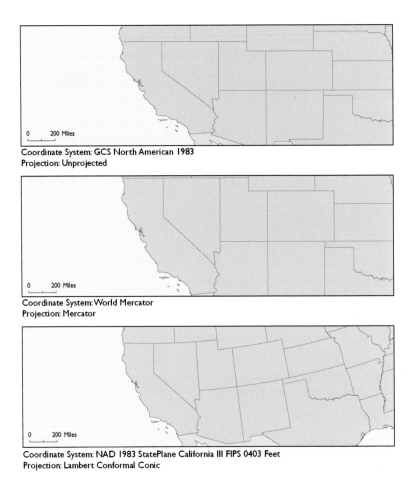

Coordinate System: GCS North American 1983
Projection: Unprojected

Coordinate System: World Mercator
Projection: Mercator

Coordinate System: NAD 1983 StatePlane California III FIPS 0403 Feet
Projection: Lambert Conformal Conic

Figure 3.1   Three projection systems showing the western United States.

using these maps. Figure 3.1 shows the western United States using three different projection systems: unprojected, Mercator, and Lambert conformal conic.

Proximity analysis

Proximity analysis involves analyzing each geographic feature (e.g., points or polygons) displayed on the map in relation to other polygons adjacent or nearby. Developing an understanding of accessibility (based on geographic distance) to urban services and facilities is particularly important for social service delivery agencies that seek, for example, to minimize transportation costs.

One commonly used method of analyzing proximity is buffering. Figure 3.2 shows buffers around vector data—a point, a line, and a polygon. One can draw a buffer of a certain distance (e.g., half-mile, one mile) around a geographic feature like a Head Start center (point) or a park. Map 3.10 shows areas within walking distance (a half-mile) of Head Start centers in San Francisco. Once buffers are identified one can calculate summary statistics for each of the buffers. Using the information produced in GIS one can create tables showing the number of children under 5 in poverty within a half-mile of a Head Start center (demonstrated in exercise 3). These types of analyses are tremendously useful in identifying any geographic gaps in coverage that may exist in cities.

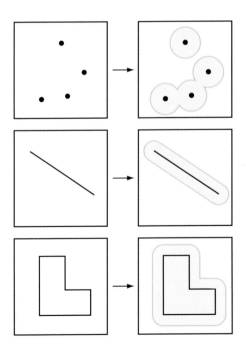

Figure 3.2   Buffering with vector data.

Map 3.10 Areas within half-mile walking distances of Head Start centers in San Francisco, 2001.

Data sources: Census 2000 TIGER/Line data down to the block group level; center locations from the San Francisco Head Start program at San Francisco State University.

The San Francisco Planning Department provided an excellent example of buffering analysis in assessing the availability of open space in San Francisco's downtown neighborhoods. The city has established the goal that every neighborhood be within a short walk to a neighborhood park. More specifically, the goal is to provide one acre of open space per one thousand households. Areas of the city where this condition is not met require priority attention in acquiring open space. In addition to an appropriate amount of open space, proximity of open space to residents is also desired. The basic standard requires that every area zoned for residential or a mix of residential and other uses must be no more than a ten-minute walk (one-quarter of a mile) from a park that is larger than one acre or very close (within one-eighth of a mile) of open space that is at least one-quarter acre. The results of the buffer analysis are shown in map 3.11. It shows existing parks and neighborhoods these parks serve. Parcels outside of these service areas and primarily residential (small, yellow polygons on map 3.11) are high-priority areas for new park acquisition. This analysis provides focus for the city and county government of San Francisco in the challenging task

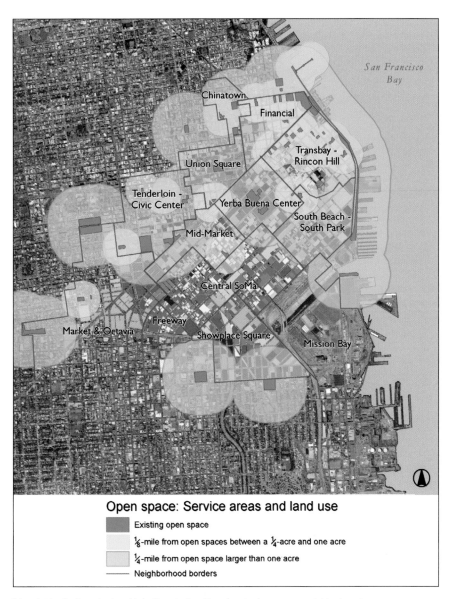

Map 3.11   Park analysis with buffers in San Francisco's downtown neighborhoods.

Source: Existing open spaces and land use with buffers, AnMarie Rodgers. © San Francisco Planning Department, Citywide Policy and Analysis.

of identifying vacant parcels for acquisition and use as open space in a built-out area like downtown San Francisco.

Another proximity analysis method involves building Thiessen polygons to determine the area of influence for facilities (e.g., Head Start centers). Child-care centers (points) can be analyzed by growing polygons around them to show "regions of influence" (DeMers 2005, 281). Assuming each point has an equal magnitude of influence, one can use the distance information between points to construct Thiessen polygons. Polygons are constructed in such a way that each location is closer to the point encircled than any other point in the study area. The exclusive area of each point is called *proximal region* (DeMers 2005, 282). Map 3.12 shows Thiessen polygons constructed around Head Start centers in San Francisco. This is an example of how GIS enables proximity analysis of child-care centers for different demographic groups by taking into account information from all of the centers in the city. The larger polygons (in area) indicate less well-served areas of the city. For example, notice the areas in the western part of the city where polygons are largest; these are underserved areas. Using GIS one can identify areas that are not well-served by existing centers and that contain large numbers of poor children—potential areas for locating a new center. One can also take center capacity into account (i.e., the number of slots available to serve eligible children in each center) to better identify underserved areas.

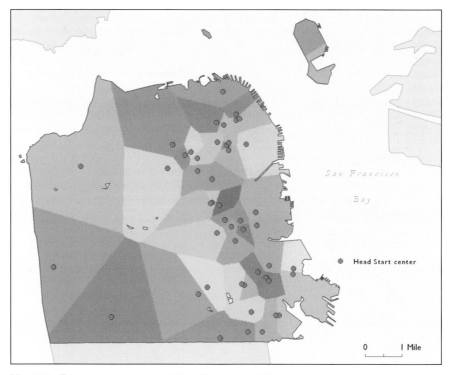

Map 3.12   Thiessen polygons around Head Start centers in San Francisco.

Data source: Center locations from the San Francisco Head Start program at San Francisco State University.

Proximity analysis with buffers and Thiessen polygons is powerful when physical accessibility (distance) is used as criteria in deciding where new centers or urban parks should be located to serve unmet needs. A more powerful method—multilayer analysis—incorporates additional variables into decision making. Multilayer analysis can work either with vector or raster data. Using vector data, as discussed in chapter 1, layers can be stacked on top of each other *(figure 1.11)*. When using raster data, the overlapping zones are assigned values (scores) as a function of each of the individual layers. For example, a data layer representing the number of poor children can be combined with another data layer representing the distances from Head Start centers. The user can assign scores (weights) to different values, which can then later be added to calculate a score for each cell of the data layer. Figure 3.3 shows an example of raster calculation. Using this method one can identify suitable locations for new Head Start centers (demonstrated in exercise 4).

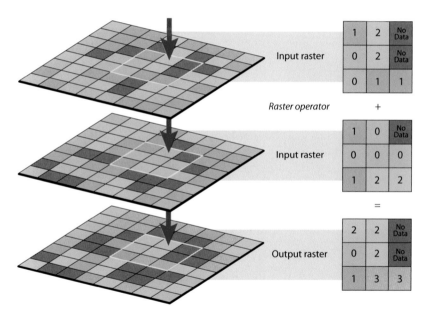

Figure 3.3   Raster calculation.

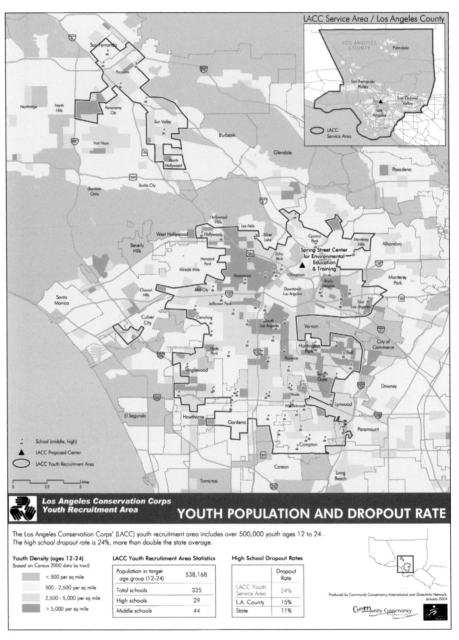

Map 3.13 Youth population and dropout rate in the greater Los Angeles area.

Source: GreenInfo Network.

Finally, advocacy groups use GIS maps to combine information and analysis in ways to make persuasive arguments and inform public policy making. The GreenInfo Network, a San Francisco-based nonprofit organization, called this approach persuasive advocacy *(www.greeninfo.org)*. The organization created map 3.13 for the Los Angeles Conservation Corps. It shows youth concentrations in Los Angeles County and summary dropout statistics. Youth recruitment areas are delineated clearly to help focus the efforts of the Conservation Corps in their work. Darker areas on the map represent areas with the highest concentrations of young people ages 12 to 24.

As discussed in this chapter, local government agencies and nonprofits can benefit from GIS analysis to carry out their functions. Examples featured in this chapter are at the forefront of innovative applications of GIS. The municipality of Rio de Janeiro's use of GIS to analyze favela settlements and social conditions of favelados with census data is a noteworthy use of GIS in a developing country setting. The use of GIS by the French regional planning agency IAURIF to document spatial concentrations of different immigrant groups in the Paris metropolitan region is an exemplary application from Europe. The use of GIS to analyze neighborhood-serving parks in San Francisco's downtown neighborhoods by the San Francisco Planning Department is strong in its analytical use of buffering with GIS. The analytical use of GIS by GreenInfo Network to inform policy making is another outstanding application. Together these examples demonstrate that urban planners worldwide are using GIS in novel ways to address unique local planning and management challenges. Social service agencies can also benefit from GIS analysis. The next chapter will discuss applications of GIS and spatial analyses that can benefit social service delivery agencies that focus on children in poverty with an emphasis on the spatial distribution of children in poverty in relation to Head Start centers in San Francisco.

Notes

1   Authorized under Title II of the Cranston-Gonzales National Affordable Housing Act (1990), HOME Investment Partnerships Program (HOME) is a federal block grant program that provides funds for state and local governments to create affordable housing for low-income households.

2   A *charette* is an interactive and participatory forum for debate where stakeholders can voice their views on a community planning problem. It enables participants to focus on a problem over half a day, a day, or a week, while also allowing them to work in groups and come up with solutions. It is a widely used method to elicit input from stakeholders in a wide range

of community planning projects that require citizen participation. It is also widely used among urban designers and architects in project conceptualization.

3   The Favela-Bairro program was launched in 1993 by the municipality of Rio de Janeiro funded by Inter-American Development Bank to improve living conditions in favelas and to integrate favelas into the rest of the city. The program seeks (1) to provide favela neighborhoods with basic sanitation services at acceptable standards; (2) to spatially reconfigure favela settlements to better integrate them with surrounding city streets; (3) to provide social services to residents; and (4) to legalize land tenure. In 2000, nearly 20 percent of the population in the municipality of Rio de Janeiro lived in favelas.

Chapter **4**

GIS analysis in planning social service delivery

The ability of a social service agency to provide accessible child-care facilities in cities requires an understanding of the spatial distribution of children in poverty. The availability of geographically referenced U.S. Census data on families with children (by income, race, and Hispanic origin) combined with geographic information systems analysis makes it possible for child-care policy officials to better understand unmet needs of families with young children. GIS applications are little known and used in human, health, and social services although it is a growing area (Queralt and Witte 1998; Haithcoat et al. 2001).

This chapter discusses how social service program delivery and planning can benefit from applications of spatial analysis methods. More often than not, community needs assessment studies carried out by government agencies and nonprofit groups lack spatial analyses even though knowledge about physical access to services can play an important role in program design. This chapter makes a case that GIS and spatial analyses can help social service providers do their jobs better. First, an overview of child-care policy issues concerned with children in poverty is provided. Second, a discussion of how GIS can be used as a tool in planning social service programs follows. Third, San Francisco's geographically referenced data is used as an illustration to show the use of GIS in locating poor children and child-care centers in San Francisco. This information is used in identifying any spatial mismatches between the need for child-care services and the supply of Head Start centers.

Children and poverty

Child poverty emerged as an important public policy concern needing urgent attention in the United States in the 1960s. The Economic Opportunity Act (War on Poverty) authorized Head Start in 1964 to address the developmental needs of poor children under 5 (Zigler and Muenchow 1992; Zigler and Valentine 1979). Head Start aims to promote social competence and school readiness by providing comprehensive developmental services for low-income preschool children and social services for their families. Early childhood education programs, such as Head Start, are key components to helping children overcome adversity early on and provide compensatory treatment for poor children. Research shows that access to quality early child education services can have both short- and long-term effects, particularly on poor children (Barnett and Boocock 1988; Currie 2001; Hill and Sandfort 1995).

Research on early childhood development shows that the well-being of children early in life determines their chances of educational, behavioral, and economic success later in adulthood (see Hill and Sandfort 1995 for a review). Many factors affect child well-being, including family-level processes such as parental beliefs and child-rearing practices, demographic characteristics and economic resources of the family, and language spoken at home (figure 4.1). These factors also influence the type of child-care selection by families (e.g., center-based child care) (Clarke-Stewart and Allhusen 2005).

Equally important is the quality of life in neighborhoods. Neighborhood institutions (e.g., schools) and neighbors can affect how a child interacts socially. Neighborhoods shape the "opportunity structure" that children face (Galster and Killen 1995). Research shows that children growing up in affluent neighborhoods mostly do better than children in low-income neighborhoods. Brooks-Gunn et al. (1993) have found significant neighborhood effects—particularly the effects of the presence of affluent neighbors—on childhood IQ, teenage births, and drop-out rates, after other socioeconomic characteristics are taken into account.

Educational psychologists and sociologists have produced much of the empirical research on the effects of the neighborhood context on child and youth development. Duncan and Raudenbush (1999) discuss methodological challenges researchers have to confront in their efforts to isolate the effects of many variables on child development. Studies using different methods have produced conflicting evidence. The literature on neighborhoods and children, for example, does not explicitly account for social service delivery institutions. Researchers who have focused on institutions such as Head Start centers, on the other hand, have shown

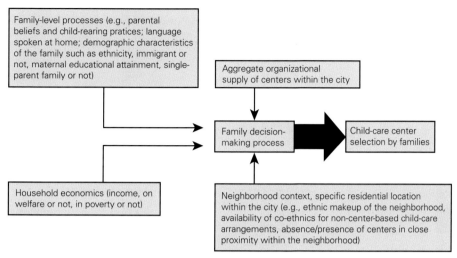

Figure 4.1 Factors influencing child-care selection by families.

that the neighborhood context within which the centers are located plays an important role in the scope and diversity of social networks reported by children attending Head Start (Bost et al. 1994). Based on their research, Bost et al. suggest that Head Start children might benefit from more "community-based" centers where social contact with families and Head Start staff may be more frequent (Bost et al. 1994, 459). Such frequency of contact can be achieved if centers are located where eligible program beneficiaries already live.

The importance of social networks and social capital for families with children is echoed by other researchers as well. Social networks fundamentally shape how children perceive opportunities later in adulthood. When low-income families live in high-poverty neighborhoods their children become subjected to distressing environmental factors during the most critical stages of their development. Because their lives and experiences are confined to a limited geographic area, children are more vulnerable to stressful events in poor neighborhoods (e.g., crime and violence) than adults. In addition, household strategies to mobilize assets in response to external shocks (e.g., loss of welfare benefits) may be constrained in isolated and impoverished neighborhoods. Households in high-poverty neighborhoods often cannot rely on resources from kin and neighbor networks to cope with and adapt to new situations, such as loss of employment, when compared to those in affluent neighborhoods (Moser 1998). For all these reasons, locating Head Start centers in close proximity to families with children in poverty is critical.

At-risk children largely live in isolation in high-poverty neighborhoods in the United States (Jargowski 1997). Hofferth (1994) and others define at-risk children as those living in low-income minority (African-American or Hispanic) families, especially in single-parent families. In the past forty years, federally funded Head Start has made great strides in helping educationally disadvantaged children who are at risk of school failure by locating its centers in city neighborhoods where the urban poor are concentrated. The analysis reported in the latter part of the chapter focuses on children in poverty living in minority family households in San Francisco down to the block group level. Access to quality early childhood educational experiences (e.g., in centers) in distressed neighborhoods where at-risk children are concentrated can play an important role in enhancing the chances of young children's success later in school.

Spatial questions concerning children and families

Increasing the accessibility of high-quality social services and facilities for families and children is a key public policy concern. Defining and measuring accessibility is complex. Access is not just a spatial phenomenon. Social, cultural, economic, and other factors can influence the accessibility of services for different groups. In spatial terms, access to opportunities in cities is not evenly distributed across different groups of people. As mentioned above, families face different opportunities in different city neighborhoods. GIS analysis can shed light on the above factors, but it is best designed to work with the geographic definition of accessibility based on physical distance. For example, using GIS, one can consider two types of location information about child-care centers—absolute and relative location. Information regarding the absolute location of child-care centers in a city (or on earth, for that matter) is useful for local child-care resource and referral agencies advising families to travel the shortest route to particular centers. Information regarding the relative location of child-care centers in relation to other centers in the city is useful in identifying "spheres of influence" or "service areas" of all of the centers. The latter type of analysis method (with Theissen polygons) is particularly useful for identifying less well-served areas of the city *(map 3.12 in chapter 3)*.

Case study background

Some of the results reported in the rest of this chapter were produced using GIS while I assisted the San Francisco Head Start Program in completing a community assessment study in 2001–2002. These are required by the U.S. Department of Health and Human Services every three years for continuation of funding. GIS was used to analyze 2000 Census data on population by age, income, race, and Hispanic origin. The GIS analysis of San Francisco's demographics answered questions such as: Where are San Francisco's children under 5 in poverty by race and Hispanic origin located? Where do single-parent female households live in the city? This analysis showed the magnitude and spatial distribution of need for Head Start services. Then, the analysis showed the spatial distribution of existing Head Start centers and contracted Head Start partners funded by the San Francisco Head Start Program—the *supply*. It showed where in the city there was unmet need in 2000 that could be filled by new Head Start centers in the future.

Measuring poverty

Because Head Start serves children in poverty, census data was analyzed with GIS to show geographic concentrations of children in poverty in San Francisco. Researchers and policy-makers in the United States use different measures of poverty. Some researchers question the use of income alone as a measure of poverty and argue for an approach that recognizes the multidimensional aspects of poverty. In international studies of urban poverty a distinction is made between *levels of poverty* and types of *vulnerability* (Moser 1998). Nonetheless, the most commonly used measure in the United States is *pretax cash income* using the official poverty threshold as a benchmark. Poverty statistics reported by the U.S. Census Bureau are based on a 1964 Social Security Administration definition, which was subsequently modified by federal interagency committees. The current definition is derived from the 1961 economy food plan (designed by the U.S. Department of Agriculture), which specifies the least costly meal for one person multiplied by three to include the cost of nonfood items (Huston et al. 1994; Reed and Van Swearingen November 2001). The cost of the economy food plan is adjusted for family size, family composition, and inflation on an annual basis. At present, the Census Bureau uses poverty thresholds that vary by family size and composition that are set by an Office of Management and Budget statistical policy directive. The official federal poverty threshold calculation considers money income before taxes. It does not include noncash benefits (e.g., public housing, Medicaid, and food stamps). In 2000, the poverty threshold for a family of three was $14,150. Those families earning at or below the poverty threshold were defined as living in poverty and eligible for public assistance. Official poverty thresholds do not vary geographically across the United States. It is an absolute number published by the U.S. Census Bureau *(www.census.gov/prod/ cen2000/doc/sf3.pdf)*.

Because the cost of living is significantly higher in cities like San Francisco, researchers and policymakers have questioned the usefulness of the federal poverty rate in high-cost cities and have argued for the use of *relative* poverty rates. One measure of *relative* poverty rate used by social service providers in California (e.g., California Department of Education, Child Development Division) specifies the poverty threshold as 75 percent of state median family income. According to state guidelines, the poverty threshold in 2000 was $35,100 for a family of three. There are many more families living in poverty when the state poverty threshold is used—26.2 percent. Researchers have also developed regionally adjusted (local) poverty thresholds that take into account housing costs (Reed and Van Swearingen November 2001). Because households spend a large share of their income on housing in San Francisco, such a regionally adjusted measure would show significantly greater numbers of families in need of government assistance. By the official federal poverty threshold, the family poverty rate in San Francisco was 9.5 percent in 2000. Following is a discussion of the results of spatial analysis of the incidence of child poverty in San Francisco by race and Hispanic origin using the federal poverty threshold.

Children in poverty in San Francisco, 1990–2000

The 2000 Census reported a total of 3,926 children under 5 in poverty in San Francisco—2,176 fewer than in 1990. The poverty rate for these children in 2000 was 13.1 percent, representing a 4.6 percentage point drop in the poverty rate since 1990 (17.7 percent). Given that San Francisco lost 11.14 percent of its *total* under-5 population between 1990 and 2000, the drop in *poor* children is disproportionately low. It suggests that families with young children who have left the city are not the poorest group. Those who leave are more likely middle-income households who prefer a larger home at an affordable price in the outlying suburbs of San Francisco to raise their young children. The cost of moving is another important factor. Because moving costs can be prohibitive for poor families, they tend to be less mobile in housing markets. Poor families who are unable to move double-up and live in overcrowded housing.

San Francisco's children in poverty live mainly in racial/ethnic minority family households. A significant percentage of all under-5 children in poverty in 2000 lived in Hispanic (30.2 percent), African-American (27.4 percent), and Asian (23.8 percent) family households. Following citywide trends, the poverty rate dropped for each major racial/ethnic minority group. For Hispanic children under 5, the poverty rate dropped from 19.7 percent in 1990 to 17.1 percent in 2000. For African-American children the drop was from 45.6 percent in 1990 to 39.6 percent in 2000. For Asian children, the Census Bureau reported a drop from 14.5 percent in 1990 to 10.1 percent in 2000. Given the economic boom in the late 1990s, the overall declining trend in poverty rates (using the official federal poverty threshold) between 1990 and 2000 is not surprising. The absolute rates of poverty for Hispanic and African-American children, however, remained at very high levels.

In addition, Hispanic and African-American children in poverty are geographically clustered in a few high-poverty neighborhoods, according to analyses with the most recent census data. Thematic mapping shows that the geographic distribution of children in poverty in San Francisco's neighborhoods is uneven. Nearly half (43.8 percent) of all children in poverty (3,926) lived in just three neighborhoods: (1) Bayview/Hunters Point (670 children); (2) Inner Mission/Bernal Heights (621 children); and (3) Visitacion Valley (427 children).

The analyses of children in poverty by race showed patterns of concentration in San Francisco's eastern neighborhoods. Hispanic children in poverty (1,185) concentrated in the Mission and the Bayview neighborhoods *(map 4.1)*. About two-thirds of African-American children in poverty (1,077) lived in the following five neighborhoods: (1) Bayview/Hunters Point (435 children); (2) Visitacion Valley (172 children); (3) Hayes Valley/Tenderloin (103 children); (4) Potrero Hill (99 children); and (5) Western Addition (77 children) *(map 4.2)*. Asian children in poverty (936) were concentrated in areas around Chinatown. About half of Asian children in poverty lived in three neighborhoods: (1) Russian Hill/Nob Hill (212 children); (2) North Beach/Telegraph Hill (129 children); and (3) Visitacion Valley (115 children) *(map 4.3)*.

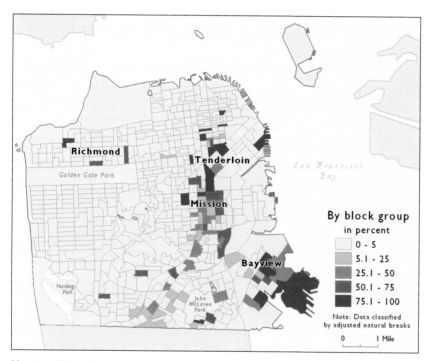

Map 4.1   Hispanic children in poverty by percent of block group, 2000.

Data sources: U.S. Census Bureau, Census 2000 Summary File 3 (SF 3), Hispanic children in poverty variable (P159H003); Census 2000 TIGER/Line data down to the census block group level.

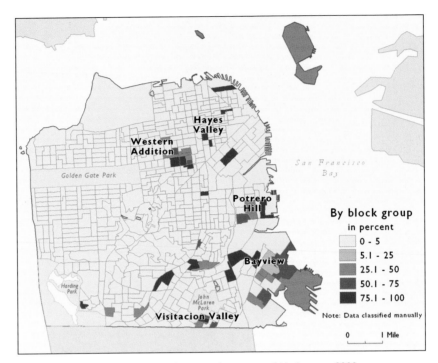

Map 4.2   African-American children in poverty by percent of block group, 2000.

Data sources: U.S. Census Bureau, Census 2000 Summary File 3 (SF 3), Hispanic children in poverty variable (P159B003); Census 2000 TIGER/Line data down to the census block group level.

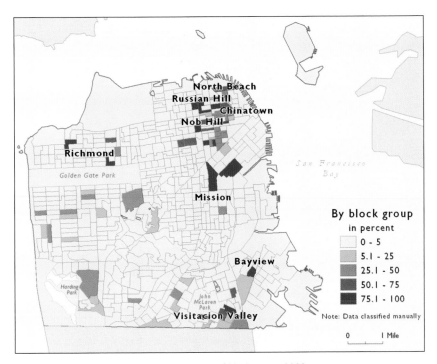

Map 4.3   Asian children in poverty by percent of block group, 2000.

Data sources: U.S. Census Bureau, Census 2000 Summary File 3 (SF 3), Hispanic children in poverty variable (P159D003);
Census 2000 TIGER/Line data down to the census block group level.

Children in poverty and Head Start center locations

Locating Head Start centers in close physical proximity to residences of poor families with
children under 5 is important for child-care providers. To better understand the physical
geography of Head Start center locations in San Francisco, proximity analysis with GIS was
carried out using buffers. Buffering analysis produced results that show children under 5
in poverty within a half-mile of each Head Start center *(map 3.10 in chapter 3)*. About one-
third of San Francisco's poor children live within walking distance of a Head Start center.
Moreover, a comparison of enrollment figures by center and poor children living within
walking distance of each center shows that many more children are living in close proximity to existing centers than slots available in these centers. For example, Ella Hill Hutch
Community Center, a grantee-operated Head Start center, in the Western Addition neighborhood, serves 71 children—only 8 percent of all poor children (875) who live within a
half-mile walking distance of this particular center[1] *(map 4.4)*. Table 4.1 shows detailed
information for another neighborhood: Inner Mission/Bernal Heights. Notice that only 3
percent of children under 5 in poverty in this neighborhood (343 out of more than 11,000)
were served by a Head Start center in 2001.

Center	Site type	Children served	Number of children within walking distance			
			All	African-American	Asian	Hispanic
Capp	Delegate Agency	80	1,308	4	65	988
Regina Chiong	Delegate Agency	80	1,486	12	35	1,166
Precita Center	Delegate Agency	40	959	17	25	648
Valencia	Delegate Agency	40	1,141	13	71	817
Mission Annex	Head Start Partner	29	1,262	6	66	876
Cesar Chavez	Head Start Partner	28	1,655	5	45	1,349
Good Samaritan	Head Start Partner	24	1,085	123	31	657
Women's Building	Delegate Agency	20	1,153	13	69	806
Dinorah Osorio	FHS FCC Provider	2	1,248	95	42	832
Total for neighborhood:		343	11,297	288	449	8,139
Note: "walking distance" is operationalized at one-half mile.						

Table 4.1   Children under 5 in poverty within walking distance of Head Start centers in Inner Mission/Bernal Heights.

Data sources: U.S. Census Bereau, Census 2000 Summary File (SF1), Census 2000 TIGER/Line data down to the census block level.

Map 4.4   Children under 5 in poverty within walking distance of the Ella Hill Hutch Community Center.

Data sources: U.S. Census Bureau, Census 2000 Summary File 3 (SF3), children under 5 in poverty variable (P087003); Census 2000 TIGER/Line data down to the block group level.

Further analysis using GIS can be carried out to identify underserved areas of the city. As discussed in chapter 1, multilayer analysis is useful when more than one criterion (variable) is considered for decision making. As shown in figure 1.11 in chapter 1, overlay analysis involves working with multiple data layers. The analysis begins by defining decision rules at the outset for locating a new center. Map 4.5 shows the results of an analysis, using raster data, where three rules were used: (1) areas had to be home to high numbers of poor children; (2) areas had to be far from existing Head Start centers and essentially under- or unserved; and (3) if areas already had Head Start centers, there needed to be under- or unserved concentrations of poor children to justify the addition of a new Head Start center. The raster data layers containing scores for each of these conditions were combined to calculate an overall score for each cell (grid). The higher values indicate areas that are most appropriate sites for opening a new center. Notice in map 4.4 that San Francisco's eastern neighborhoods are well populated by existing Head Start centers, but southeastern and western portions of the city where population gains were recorded by the 2000 Census are relatively underserved.

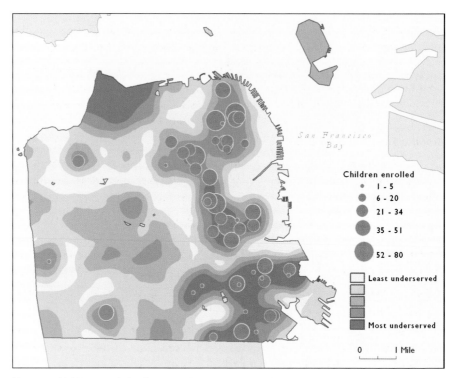

Map 4.5   Multilayer analysis of areas underserved by Head Start centers. (Note: Service level determined by number of poor children per block group. Data classified by adjusted natural breaks method.)

Data sources: U.S. Census Bureau, Census 2000 Summary File 3 (SF3), children in poverty variable (P087003); Census 2000 TIGER/Line data down to the census block group level; San Francisco Head Start program at San Francisco State University.

This chapter showed an example of GIS analysis of child demographics and child-care centers in San Francisco. It showed the GIS application of proximity analysis and multilayer analysis with Head Start center and 2000 Census data for San Francisco. It showed the advantage of using two different types of GIS data models (vector and raster) in the analysis as they revealed different types of useful information.

Buffering analysis using vector data enabled the production of useful descriptive statistics per contained area (e.g., half-mile buffer). For example, child-care service providers can determine how many children in poverty by race and Hispanic origin live within walking distance from each of the centers *(table 4.1)*. Multilayer analysis with raster data on the other hand produced results for geographic areas that can be much more fine-grained as shown in map 4.5 because cell size in GIS can be defined by the user. Raster analysis results can later be aggregated into policy-relevant social service areas or zones for planning and social delivery purposes. Raster analysis involves intensive computer computations and requires abstract thinking, but the results can be translated, with skill, into a form that can be understood and acted upon by policy makers. Exercise 4 on the CD provides the data and instructions to replicate this analysis using ArcGIS software. The key is that GIS analysis methods discussed here can provide objective analytical tools to policy makers in the child-care community. In an era of public-sector funding cutbacks, the objective and detailed analyses that GIS provides is particularly useful for program maintenance and expansion.

Chapters 3 and 4 focused on the use of GIS in urban planning and social service delivery applications. Exercises 3 and 4 on the CD demonstrate how one can carry out vector and raster analysis with ArcGIS software using Head Start center data and census data on children in poverty. Social service delivery agencies can carry out these kinds of analyses with their own data to solve public policy problems that might benefit from a spatial analysis perspective.

The next two chapters will focus on the use of spatial analysis methods to answer specific social science research questions to better manage urban development in global cities. It will show how one can use GIS to locate immigrant clusters in global cities and analyze housing conditions in neighborhoods where the foreign-born population is disproportionately concentrated. As mentioned in the introduction of this book, the analysis of immigrant population concentrations and clusters in four U.S. global metropolitan regions is aimed at contributing to our understanding of the spatial organization of metropolitan regions with global significance. As such, the last two chapters of this book will put the analytical tools covered in the book into use in providing a spatial perspective into theories of immigrant housing settlement formation.

Notes

1   For additional detailed tables and figures see Pamuk (2003).

Part **3**

Analyzing spatial patterns in metropolitan areas with GIS

Chapter 5

Locating immigrant clusters with census data

A desire to own one's home is a universal phenomenon, and it finds its expression in different ways around the world. For households in poverty in so-called third-world countries, building a roof over one's head has long required little more than identifying a piece of vacant land and getting help from friends and neighbors for construction (Turner 1977). Through a process of self-help construction and communal assistance, entire neighborhoods in the developing world were built and became established (Pamuk 1991). Cities no longer have much vacant land for recent migrants to occupy and develop through self-help construction. Instead, existing squatter settlements in central locations now have high densities *(figures 1.5 and 1.6 in chapter 1),* and the newcomers rent or buy existing units in these types of neighborhoods (Pamuk 1996; Keyder 2005). As discussed in the introduction of this book, these settlements are known as informal housing settlements, heavily populated by migrants from rural areas who are unable to afford housing in planned subdivisions.

Municipal assistance to informal housing settlements often comes, if at all, after the neighborhoods have been established—as a response to substandard living conditions—like in the case of Rio de Janeiro's Favela-Bairro program mentioned in chapter 3 (Pamuk and Cavallieri 1998). Squatter upgrading programs provide basic infrastructure such as roads, drainage, and sewerage to neighborhoods built in haste without necessary building approvals. In addition, services such as water and electricity are provided. The upgrading process involves eventually granting residents legal title to the piece of land they have occupied illegally and to the house they have built on that land. Informal housing settlements at substandard quality are very visible in megacities in the developing world like São Paulo and Mexico City, and provide evidence of the tremendous challenges that municipalities face in managing urbanization. Rapid migration from rural areas to major cities continues to fuel the growth of informal housing settlements.

Global cities in the United States and western Europe face a different set of urban management challenges. Because legal and financial markets are highly developed and urban planning follows a sequence of building permit approval first and occupancy next, poorer households in these regions do not attempt to build houses on occupied land without building permits. Instead, households in poverty in the United States end up geographically concentrated in less desirable locations—mostly older rental housing left by the more affluent—of metropolitan areas (Briggs 2005). This process of "filtering" housing to the urban poor takes place as affluent households move increasingly farther out to the suburbs and exurbs. As Myron Orfield's community classification shows, affluent job centers in the United States are now located outside of traditional central cities (Orfield 2002; *map i* in the introduction). In contrast, the strength and dynamism of European cities lie in their centers (Le Gales 2002, 28). European governments have built social housing developments at the outskirts of major cities[1] like Paris and Amsterdam, which are now primarily inhabited by immigrant populations *(map 1.4 in chapter 1)*.

Today, the geography of global metropolitan regions and housing markets are significantly affected by immigration flows from abroad. In the United States and western Europe, most middle-income households can attain homeownership through long-term mortgage financing, except in very expensive housing markets. Nearly 70 percent of U.S. households are homeowners (Joint Center for Housing Studies of Harvard University 2005), and more than half of the total housing stock in western European countries are occupied by owners. The attractiveness of certain metropolitan areas, however, combined with other factors results in the escalation of housing prices, making homeownership beyond the reach for many in these areas. Global metropolitan housing markets—the focus of this book—are especially difficult markets for attaining homeownership for moderate and low-income households. In London, San Francisco, and Amsterdam a large share of the housing stock is occupied by renters—41 percent, 65 percent, and 83 percent, respectively *(www.iut.nu)*. The complex interplay of many different factors contributes to this outcome, which is discussed in the following pages. This chapter will examine the relationship among the demographics of the immigrant populations, their residential location decisions, and housing market dynamics in global metropolitan regions.

To begin understanding the spatial distribution of immigrant populations, two core analytic concepts are useful—*clustering and dispersal* (Pamuk 2004). A clustered spatial pattern is one where the observed phenomenon (in this case immigrant populations) is found to be disproportionately higher in a geographic entity (e.g., census tract) when compared to the larger reference area (e.g., MSA). The clustered pattern is captured as a snapshot of the spatial distribution of a phenomenon at a particular time and place. The concept of dispersal, on the other hand, involves a temporal dimension and describes a changing spatial pattern of the phenomenon over time, say fifty years *(figure 5.1)*. As noted earlier in the book's introduction, spatial clustering patterns of immigrants was first noted by Chicago School sociologists who observed this phenomenon during the course of their research focusing on Chicago's neighborhoods in the 1920s. In their theory, now known as the human ecology approach, cities develop through a process of competition among households for space that ultimately gives rise to homogenous concentric zones (Burgess 1925) *(figure ii in introduction)*. According to this theory, new ethnic groups are first expected to live in congested conditions in *zones-in-transition* but move later to *working-class districts* (and eventually disperse into the mainstream housing market) soon after their socioeconomic situation improves.

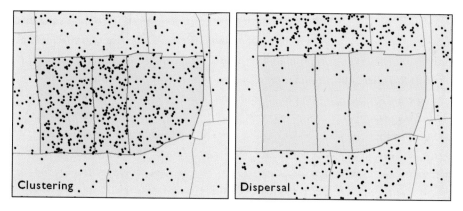

Figure 5.1   Clustering and dispersal.

More recently, changing patterns of ethnic residential clustering and the functioning of ethnic economies in the United States have also captured the scholarly attention of economic sociologists devoted to analyzing the assimilation of immigrants and ethnic entrepreneurship; these areas of inquiry provide rich empirical evidence for understanding socially oriented economic action (Portes and Sensenbrenner 1993). This interest has spawned a rich literature. Portes, one of the key thinkers in this area, defines ethnic clusters as "spatially clustered networks of businesses owned by owners of the same minority" (Portes 1995, 27). In a similar vein, Alba et al. (1997) define ethnic neighborhoods as areas where an immigrant group is concentrated along with an "ethnic institutional infrastructure," such as stores selling ethnic products (Alba et al. 1997, 886). There is increasing evidence that immigrants are drawn to ethnic neighborhoods because of the rich social and institutional infrastructure that responds to quality-of-life needs that are transnational in scope and unavailable elsewhere. As another growing scholarly field on transnationalism, flexible citizenship, and ethnic identity suggests, contemporary immigrant neighborhoods are becoming places where new narratives are written and solutions devised in the formation of distinct identities (Smith 2001; Ong 1999). Tolerance for immigrants by the native-born population in the United States has further nurtured the rise of multiethnic neighborhoods and cities. As Florida (2002) has argued, the convergence of technology, talent, and tolerance (particularly for immigrants) in cities like San Francisco, Boston, Seattle, and Los Angeles has been especially beneficial in spurring creativity and economic growth.

Defining an immigrant cluster with GIS

GIS methods are helpful in understanding spatial clustering patterns of immigrants (Pamuk 2004; Logan and Zhang 2004). Building on research by Logan et al. (2002), an immigrant cluster here is defined as a set of *contiguous* tracts that contain at least one tract with an immigrant concentration (core) of at least 10 percentage points above the reference area's (e.g., MSA) average for that immigrant group. The other tracts in the cluster have an immigrant concentration of at least 5 percentage points above the reference area's average for that immigrant group. (Figure 5.2 is a schematic that illustrates these principles.) The levels of immigrant *concentrations* can be identified using GIS, and census tracts that are contiguous to one another can be marked manually. With the assistance of my research associates, I have done this for each of the three metropolitan regions using ArcGIS software (this chapter reports analysis results for San Francisco at the city and county level only). Following the identification and marking of immigrant clusters using GIS, I labeled each of the clusters based on key-informant interviews with those familiar with the local geography of ethnic neighborhoods in the three regions (analysis results for the nine-county San Francisco Bay Area, New York MSA, and Los Angeles MSA are reported in chapter 6). An Internet search was also carried out to identify names used for these clusters by local community organizations and groups themselves. These datasets and one additional MSA (Washington, D.C.) are available for analysis in the self-directed project on the CD. The process of identifying immigrant clusters and labeling them in GIS is demonstrated in exercise 5.

After identifying, marking, and mapping immigrant clusters, I compared selected housing conditions in immigrant cluster neighborhoods to nonimmigrant neighborhoods.

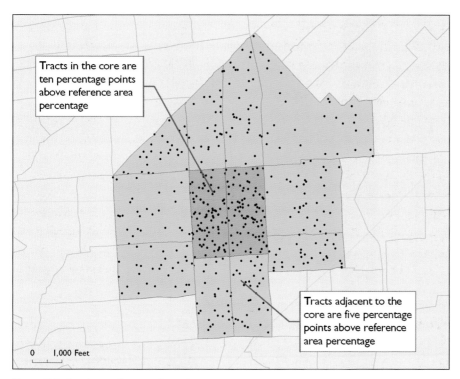

Figure 5.2   Immigrant clusters schematic.

Three key housing market outcome measures were used: homeownership, housing cost burden, and overcrowding. The census variables used to measure these include the percentage of households who are homeowners, the percentage of households who pay more than 50 percent of their income on housing, and the percentage of households who are living in overcrowded conditions (more than one occupant per room). Linguistic isolation and year of entry were used as indicators of assimilation.

Identifying spatial clustering patterns of immigrants in global metropolitan regions using GIS is driven by two analytical motivations: (1) to examine the variation of immigrant clusters in spatial terms (shape, size, morphology), and; (2) to examine the extent to which housing conditions significantly differ inside and outside of clusters. If the analysis shows that households in immigrant clusters are more likely to live in overcrowded dwelling units, less likely to achieve homeownership, and more likely to experience housing cost burdens, then designing new policies to remedy these conditions would be desirable. If these patterns are consistently present in the three metropolitan regions (discussed in chapter 6), we can establish strong empirical evidence to better depict the actual housing conditions of immigrants in contemporary urban America.

Furthermore, with the analysis of immigrant clusters using 2000 Census data and GIS analysis, one can establish the empirical foundation to ask the following questions: Where are immigrant clusters located? How do housing outcomes vary inside and outside of clusters? To what extent is membership in an immigrant cluster associated with rates of homeownership, cost burden, and overcrowding? Analysis of data at the aggregate census tract level allows us to ask questions such as: Are China-born clusters more likely to be comprised of high homeownership tracts? Are Mexico-born clusters more likely to be comprised of overcrowded tracts?

It is important to note that the analysis reported here is at the census tract level rather than at the household level, which means that inferences from aggregate census tract level data to household level should be made with caution in order to avoid modifiable area unit and ecological fallacy problems (discussed in chapter 3). As I have done (Pamuk 2004), researchers should use multiple methods (including ethnographic research) and multiple data sources to confirm the actual spatial distribution of the population being studied within the tracts and report analysis of aggregate census data for tracts with care.

In the following analysis the terms China-born, Mexico-born, and Philippines-born are used to describe only foreign-born people, even though they may have been living in the United States for many years. These terms and the analyses do not include people born in the United States to foreign-born parents (they are counted in the census by another variable: ancestry in the census questionnaire). References related to those of Chinese, Mexican, and Filipino descent are based on ethnographic research reported in the literature.

San Francisco's Hispanic population and its Mexico-born cluster

In 2000, Hispanics comprised 14.1 percent of San Francisco's population. Between 1990 and 2000, San Francisco gained 8,797 residents of Hispanic origin. Hispanics are concentrated in the Mission District along a major north-south artery (Mission Street) *(map 5.1)*. Between 1990 and 2000, Hispanics have moved into more affordable southern parts of the city. Nearly 60 percent of San Francisco's Hispanics live within a foreign-born cluster *(table 5.1)*. Forty-six percent of the Mexico-born population lives in the city's Mexico-born cluster *(table 5.2)*.

San Francisco's Mexico-born population is sizable: it comprises 21 percent of all Hispanics in the city while people from El Salvador comprise 13 percent, and those from Nicaragua 6.8 percent of all Hispanics. The Mexico-born population selected for this analysis is clustered in the Mission District *(map 5.2)*. The Mexico-born cluster can be characterized as a traditional ethnic *enclave* in the original sense of the term, in which low-income, working-class immigrants are concentrated in a neighborhood—in this case in the Mission District.

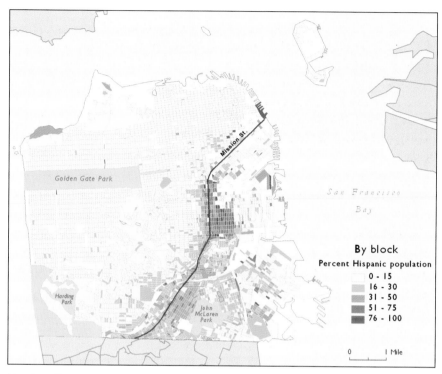

Map 5.1   Hispanic population in San Francisco, 2000. (Note: White indicates no data. Data classified manually.)

Data sources: U.S. Census Bureau, Census 2000 Summary File 1 (SF 1), Hispanic population variable (P008010); Census 2000 TIGER/Line data down to the census block level.

Ethnic group and characteristics	Within foreign-born clusters	Outside of foreign-born clusters
Foreign-born (immigrant) population		
Number of census tracts	63	113
Number of foreign-born	116,660	118,881
Hispanics		
Number of Hispanics	64,165	45,339
Percent city's Hispanics	58.6	41.4
Mean percent Hispanics	20.6	10.4
Asians		
Number of Asians	145,543	94,022
Percent city's Asians	60.8	39.3
Mean percent Asians	46.1	19.4
Note: Foreign-born persons comprise 36.8 percent of the county's total population. An immigrant cluster area is defined as a set of contiguous tracts, that contain at least one tract in which a group has a level of concentration of at least ten percentage points above the county's average (46.8 percent) and whose other tracts have a level of concentration of at least five percentage points above the county's average (41.8 percent).		

Table 5.1   Distribution of major ethnic groups across immigrant and nonimmigrant cluster areas.

a. Foreign-born		
Ethnic group and characteristics	Within foreign-born clusters	Outside of foreign-born clusters

Foreign-born
  Number of census tracts
  Number of foreign-born
  Percent city's foreign-born
  Mean percent foreign-born
	63
	166,660
	58.4
	52.5
		113
		118,881
		41.6
		25.4

b. Mexico-born		
Ethnic group and characteristics	Within Mexico-born clusters	Outside of Mexico-born clusters

Mexico-born clusters
  Number of census tracts
  Number of Mexico-born
  Percent city's Mexico-born
  Mean percent Mexico-born
	14
	10,575
	46.1
	15.2
		162
		12,341
		53.9
		4.8

c. Philippines-born		
Ethnic group and characteristics	Within Philippines-born clusters	Outside of Philippines-born clusters

Philippines-born
  Number of census tracts
  Number of Philippines-born
  Percent city's Philippines-born
  Mean percent Philippines-born
	22
	14,450
	45.9
	14.2
		154
		17,006
		54.1
		4.5

d. China-born		
Ethnic group and characteristics	Within China-born clusters	Outside of China-born clusters

China-born
  Number of census tracts
  Number of China-born
  Percent city's China-born
  Mean percent China-born
	35
	52,685
	54.6
	31.8
		141
		43,889
		45.4
		9.9

Note: There are four types of immigrant clusters: Foreign-born clusters, China-born clusters, Philippines-born clusters, and Mexico-born clusters. The clusters are defined as a set of contiguous tracts, that contain at least one tract where a group is represented at a rate 10 percentage points above the group's share in the total population and whose other tracts each have an immigrant concentration level of at least 41.8 percent for foreign-born clusters, 17.4 percent for China-born clusters, 9 percent for Philippines-born clusters, and 8 percent for Mexico-born clusters.

Table 5.2   Distribution of the immigrant population across different types of immigrant clusters.

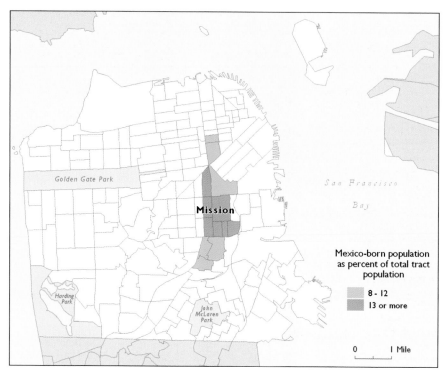

Map 5.2 Mexico-born cluster in San Francisco, 2000. (Note: Mexico-born persons comprise 3 percent of the county's total population. White indicates areas without any clusters.)

Data sources: U.S. Census Bureau, Census 2000 Summary File 3 (SF 3), Mexico-born population variable (PCT19103); Census 2000 TIGER/Line data down to the census tract level.

The neighborhood has a vibrant identifiable ethnic economy and social infrastructure that serves not just the Mexico-born population but also the broader Latino community, including people from El Salvador and Nicaragua.

Historically, the Mission District has housed waves of different ethnic groups. Following the Spanish Mission settlement in 1776, it became home to Italian, Irish, German, and Scandinavian immigrants in the nineteenth century who were then displaced by the 1906 earthquake and fire. The 1940s and 1950s saw the emigration of working-class residents from this neighborhood to the suburbs, leaving much of the housing stock to new immigrants from Central and South America, many of whom had been previously displaced by civil wars in their homelands. In the 1980s, young middle-class professionals moved into the area, but as Castells (1983) notes, the neighborhood remained the *barrio* (the Latino ghetto) of the city throughout the 1980s. Much like Chinatown, which displays the Asian roots of San Francisco, the Mission District embodies the city's Latin American heritage (Castells 1983).

Mexico-born		
Ethnic group and characteristics	Within Mexico-born clusters	Outside of Mexico-born clusters
Mexico-born clusters		
Mean percent overcrowded		
owner occupied, more than 1 occupant per room	13.4	10.6
owner occupied, more than 1.5 occupants per room	7.4	6.1
renter occupied, more than 1 occupant per room	29.2**	15.4**
renter occupied, more than 1.5 occupants per room	20.7**	9.9**
Mean percent cost burdened (>50 percent of income spent on rent)	17.1	16.2
Mean percent homeownership	23.4**	39.2**
Mean percent without kitchen	4.8	3.6
Mean percent in poverty	17.7**	11.1**
Mean percent year of entry		
1990 to March 2000	42.9**	36.0**
1965 to 1989	50.0	52.3
before 1965	7.0**	11.7**
Mean percent resided in a foreign country, 1995	9.5**	6.2**
Average median household income	48,393*	59,946*
Mean percent linguistically isolated		
Spanish-speaking households	33.4**	16.3**
*p < .10, **p < .05 (two-tail test)		

Note: Differences in average median household income among census tracts within Mexico-born clusters (left column) and census tracts outside of Mexico-born clusters (right column) in San Francisco are marginally significant (p < .10). We note more robust differences (p <.05) in mean percent homeownership.

  Notice that average median household income within Mexico-born clusters (left column) is $48,393. The average median household income outside of Mexico-born clusters (right column) is $59,946. The difference ($11,553) is statistically significant (p < .10). In other words, the difference could not have happened by chance alone. The probability of the difference occurring by chance (due to sampling error) is less than 10 percent. Therefore, we can conclude that average median household income within Mexico-born clusters is lower when compared to the rest of the region.

  Similarly, mean homeownership within Mexico-born clusters (left column) is 23.4 percent. Mean homeownership outside of Mexico-born clusters (right column) is 39.2 percent. The difference (15.8 percent) is statistically significant (p < .05). Therefore, we can conclude that rates of homeownership within Mexico-born clusters are lower when compared to the rest of the region.

  In summary, areas where Mexico-born population is concentrated have lower household incomes and lower rates of homeownership when compared to the rest of the region.

> **Also note:** There are four types of immigrant clusters: Foreign-born clusters, China-born clusters, Philippines-born clusters, and Mexico-born clusters. The clusters are defined as a set of contiguous tracts, which contain at least one tract where a group is represented at a rate 10 percentage points above the group's share in the total population and whose other tracts each have an immigrant concentration level of at least 41.8 percent for foreign-born clusters, 17.4 percent for China-born clusters, 9 percent for Philippines-born clusters, and 8 percent for Mexico-born clusters.

Table 5.3   Differences within and outside of Mexico-born clusters.

Table 5.3 compares selected housing and socioeconomic conditions inside and outside of Mexico-born clusters. Overall, renter-occupied dwelling units in the Mexico-born cluster are more likely to be overcrowded when compared to the rest of the city. On average, 29.2 percent of the dwelling units occupied by renters in the Mexico-born cluster are overcrowded (more than one person per room), compared with units occupied by renters in the rest of the city (15.4 percent).

Unlike the China-born and the Philippines-born clusters (discussed later), homeownership is less common within the Mexico-born cluster. On average, just 23.4 percent of units are occupied by owners within the Mexico-born cluster, compared with 39.2 percent in the rest of the city. On average, the median household income is lower in the Mexico-born cluster ($48,393), compared with the median income of households in the rest of the city ($59,946). These findings are consistent with the spatial assimilation theory, which posits that immigrants who are economically better off are found outside of ethnic clusters. Furthermore, a significant percentage of the foreign-born population living in the Mexico-born cluster is recent immigrants who have entered the U.S. between 1990 and 2000 (42.9 percent), compared to others in the rest of the city (36 percent). Overall, the Mexico-born cluster displays characteristics that fit the ethnic *enclave* model better than either the Philippines-born or the China-born clusters. The Mexico-born cluster has also faced the greatest pressure of change in the city throughout the 1990s urban redevelopment activity.

San Francisco's Asian population and its China-born and Philippines-born clusters

In 2000, there were many more Asians in San Francisco (239,564) than African-Americans and Hispanics combined. Between 1990 and 2000, San Francisco gained 48,874 Asian/Pacific Islanders. Map 5.3 shows the distribution of the Asian population in 2000. A significant share of the Asian population is comprised of China-born persons. In 2000, there were nearly 100,000 China-born persons in San Francisco (13 percent of the total population, 35 percent of the foreign-born population, and 45 percent of all Asians).

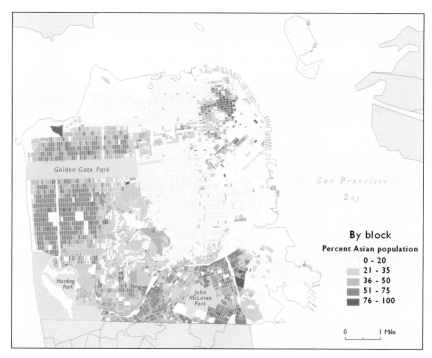

Map 5.3 Asian population in San Francisco, 2000. (Note: White indicates no data. Data classified manually.)

Data sources: U.S. Census Bureau, Census 2000 Summary File 1 (SF 1), Asian population variable (P007005); Census 2000 TIGER/Line data down to the census block level.

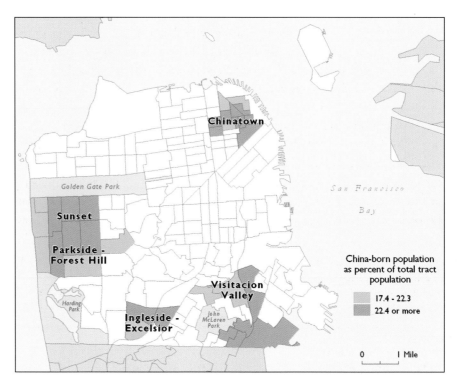

Map 5.4 China-born clusters in San Francisco, 2000. (Note: China-born persons comprise 12.4 percent of the county's total population. White indicates areas without any clusters.)

Data sources: U.S. Census Bureau, Census 2000 Summary File 3 (SF 3), China-born population variable (PCT19034); Census 2000 TIGER/Line data down to the census tract level.

The China-born clustering pattern is the most complex, as it takes three different forms as shown in map 5.4: the traditional enclave in Chinatown; an ethnic cluster in a relatively affluent setting in the Sunset, Parkside, and Forest Hill neighborhoods (far left); and two amorphous clusters in the southern part of the city, which includes Ingleside, Excelsior, and Visitation Valley neighborhoods. The spatial clustering patterns of the China-born do not easily fit the dual concept of ethnic neighborhoods as either ethnic enclave or ethnic community.

There continues to be a concentration of Asian and Pacific Islanders in the Chinatown area, where San Francisco's Asian population has been concentrated since the 1850s. Chinatown is characterized by very densely spaced, small rental units and has been and continues to be a point of entry for poor Asian immigrants—a traditional ethnic enclave. It is also a residential area for long-term lower-income Asians—particularly elderly or linguistically isolated Chinese-Americans. While Chinatown still had a concentration of Asians in 2000, the neighborhood actually lost population between 1990 and 2000. There was a substantial migration of Asian and Pacific Islander households into western parts of the city bordering

Golden Gate Park. This area became the new Chinese suburbs, with row housing, single-family homes, and more expensive rental housing. The two clusters in the southeastern portion of the city, on the other hand, are middle and lower-income areas that have a very small ethnic business infrastructure and a much more amorphous form in terms of a large land area.

Table 5.4 compares selected housing and socioeconomic conditions inside and outside of China-born clusters. Overall, dwelling units in China-born clusters are more likely to be overcrowded when compared to units in the non-China-born areas throughout the city. On average, 20.1 percent of the dwelling units occupied by owners in the city's China-born clusters are overcrowded (more than one person per room) when compared with units occupied by owners in the rest of the city (8.5 percent). This suggests that homeownership in areas

China-born		
Ethnic group and characteristics	Within China-born clusters	Outside of China-born clusters
China-born		
Mean percent overcrowded		
owner occupied, more than 1 occupant per room	20.1**	8.5**
owner occupied, more than 1.5 occupants per room	12.6**	4.6**
renter occupied, more than 1 occupant per room	24.0**	14.7**
renter occupied, more than 1.5 occupants per room	15.1**	9.7**
Mean percent cost burdened	18.0**	15.9**
(>50 percent of income spent on rent)		
Mean percent homeownership	46.3**	35.8**
Mean percent without kitchen	7.6**	2.7**
Mean percent in poverty	11.2	11.7
Mean percent year of entry		
1990 to March 2000	35.3	36.8
1965 to 1989	55.2**	51.3**
before 1965	9.5	11.8
Mean percent resided in a foreign country, 1995	7.6**	6.2**
Average median household income	51,573**	60,878**
Mean percent linguistically isolated		
Asian-speaking households	46.5**	30.4**
*p < .10, **p < .05 (two-tail test)		
Note: There are four types of immigrant clusters: Foreign-born clusters, China-born clusters, Philippines-born clusters, and Mexico-born clusters. The clusters are defined as a set of contiguous tracts, which contain at least one tract where a group is represented at a rate 10 percentage points above the group's share in the total population and whose other tracts each have an immigrant concentration level of at least 41.8 percent for foreign-born clusters, 17.4 percent for China-born clusters, 9 percent for Philippines-born clusters, and 8 percent for Mexico-born clusters.		

Table 5.4   Differences within and outside of China-born clusters.

where the China-born are concentrated involves extended families and that, like renters in the Mexico-born cluster, homeowners in the China-born clusters are more likely to live in housing conditions that housing planners define as overcrowded. On average, the percentage of units occupied by owners in China-born clusters (46.3 percent) is significantly higher when compared to the rest of the city (35.8 percent), which shows the desirability of this particular type of ethnic cluster for permanent settlement for the China-born. Overall, San Francisco's China-born clusters (except for Chinatown) do not seem to function as zones-in-transition for poor, uneducated, and linguistically isolated Chinese immigrants. Further analysis of China-born clusters (not shown here) by separating Chinatown from the other two main China-born clusters confirms this finding.

The settlement patterns of Filipinos have received far less attention in the literature than those of the Chinese. In 2000, Filipinos comprised the third-largest immigrant group in the city. The early wave of Filipinos arrived in the 1920s and 1930s, and was mostly male migrant farmworkers on their way to Hawaii or to California's San Joaquin Valley (Godfrey 1988, 105). These workers spent the winter in residential hotels in areas bordering Chinatown, which came to be known as Manilatown. A recent study by Laguerre (2000) details the historical factors that led to the gradual disappearance of Manilatown—the heart of the Filipino community—following the demise of anchor institutions like the International Hotel, which provided shelter and services for poor elderly Filipinos and seasonal agricultural workers. Many Filipino residents along with others were evicted in 1977 from the International Hotel, following an order issued by a Hong Kong–based investment firm that owned the hotel and had other plans for it. Filipinos who arrived following World War II are more educated and affluent than the earlier waves of immigrants and have dispersed to other parts of the city.

While spatially Filipinos also exhibit a clustering pattern, the two clusters in map 5.5 are primarily residential areas and do not have an identifiable ethnic economy like the Mission District. The broad cluster in the southeastern part of the city resembles what Alba et al. would call an ethnic *community*, in which more affluent Filipinos are spatially clustered but without the kind of rich ethnic economy that traditional ethnic enclaves have (although a vibrant ethnic Filipino economy is present in adjacent Daly City—in the neighboring San Mateo County—just south of San Francisco and not shown on the map) where businesses are located. The second Philippines-born cluster in the upper right in the map includes low-income Filipinos residing in residential hotels, along the 6th Street corridor of the South of Market neighborhood. This area houses many of the lowest-income elderly Filipinos in residential hotels and Filipino families in apartment buildings. Other poorer South East Asian groups (e.g., Cambodian and Vietnamese) live nearby in the Tenderloin neighborhood. The other Philippines-born cluster in the southeast portion of San Francisco has an

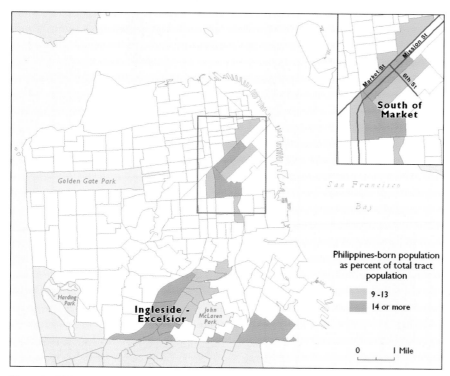

Map 5.5   Philippines-born clusters in San Francisco, 2000. (Note: Philippines-born persons comprise 4 percent of the county's total population. White indicates areas without any clusters.)

Data sources: U.S. Census Bureau, Census 2000 Summary File 3 (SF 3), Philippines-born population variable (PCT19053); Census 2000 TIGER/Line data down to the census tract level.

amorphous form. It has no distinctly identifiable ethnic economy, but is adjacent to Daly City—in neighboring San Mateo County—where Filipino businesses are located.

Table 5.5 shows that units are more likely to be occupied by owners within the Philippines-born clusters. On average, 50.3 percent of the units within a Philippines-born cluster are occupied by owners, compared with 36.1 percent in the rest of the city. Like the Chinese, Filipinos seem to express a preference for homeownership where their co-ethnics are concentrated. In New York, Logan et al. (2002, 316) has also found that the more affluent Filipinos are the more likely to live in an ethnic cluster and be homeowners.

Researchers continue to fine-tune methods to better depict the spatial distribution of immigrants and their impact on cities.[2] The GIS methods used in this chapter involved: (1) the classification of census data on the foreign-born variable to locate high concentrations; (2) the selection of contiguous and high concentration census tracts; and (3) coding to indicate the type of immigrant cluster (demonstrated in exercise 5). The resulting database was analyzed in a statistical software package (SPSS). The application of spatial analysis methods with GIS and standard nonspatial analysis methods of data with a statistical software package

Philippines-born		
Ethnic group and characteristics	Within Philippines-born clusters	Outside of Philippines-born clusters
Philippines-born		
Mean percent overcrowded		
owner occupied, more than 1 occupant per room	20.8**	9.4**
owner occupied, more than 1.5 occupants per room	11.6**	5.5**
renter occupied, more than 1 occupant per room	33.2**	14.1**
renter occupied, more than 1.5 occupants per room	22.0**	9.1**
Mean percent cost burdened	19.2**	15.9**
(>50 percent of income spent on rent)		
Mean percent homeownership	50.3**	36.1**
Mean percent without kitchen	7.0**	3.2**
Mean percent in poverty	13.3	11.4
Mean percent year of entry		
1990 to March 2000	35.8	36.6
1965 to 1989	56.7**	51.5**
before 1965	7.5**	11.9**
Mean percent resided in a foreign country, 1995	7.1	6.4
Average median household income	47,704**	60,645**
Mean percent linguistically isolated		
Asian speaking households	37.0	33.1
*p < .10, **p < .05 (two tail test)		
Note: There are four types of immigrant clusters: Foreign-born clusters, China-born clusters, Philippines-born clusters, and Mexico-born clusters. The clusters are defined as a set of contiguous tracts, which contain at least one tract where a group is represented at a rate 10 percentage points above the group's share in the total population and whose other tracts each have an immigrant concentration level of at least 41.8 percent for foreign-born clusters, 17.4 percent for China-born clusters, 9 percent for Philippines-born clusters, and 8 percent for Mexico-born clusters.		

Table 5.5   Differences within and outside of Philippines-born clusters.

enabled a stronger analysis than was possible with one tool alone. This is what had been referred to as "loosely coupled" modeling in chapter 1. The analysis of the new clustering pattern of particular immigrant groups within Asian and Hispanic groups using GIS refined our understanding of settlement patterns and housing outcomes for these groups. The spatial clustering pattern of Mexico-born in San Francisco resembles the traditional ethnic enclave model. The spatial distribution of Philippines- and China-born somewhat deviates from this model. The variations in clustering patterns are related to income, linguistic ability, access to the ethnic economy, and larger historical patterns of group assimilation.

From a public policy perspective, immigrant populations present new urban management challenges for U.S. and European city governments that are not yet fully articulated and translated into solutions and programs. Much of the discussions of immigration policy in the United States regarding who and how many people to admit into the country are at the federal level, leaving city-level impacts unaddressed. At present, the toolkit of urban planners and policy makers concerned with cities clearly needs some fresh thinking in order to successfully orchestrate different demographic groups to invent solutions to deal with low homeownership and housing quality problems. In this context, GIS can help to provide objective analysis and visualization of alternative community planning scenarios taking into account different perspectives or simply document population and housing trends using census data and maps that will inform policy. This approach can help better manage global cities with diverse populations.

This chapter discussed immigrant clustering patterns in the city and county of San Francisco. To what extent are the patterns discussed here found in other global metropolitan regions? Is San Francisco unique in successfully encouraging immigrants to create thriving and nonthreatening communities and ethnic economies (Light and Gold 2000)? For the Europeans, immigration is a relatively recent phenomenon and still fraught with much fear and anxiety (Rifkin 2004). The next chapter will discuss immigrant clustering patterns in other U.S. global metropolitan regions—New York and Los Angeles.

Notes

1   It must be noted that most of the cities in Europe are medium sized (population between 150,000 and 200,000, and 1.5 million to 2 million) (Le Gales 2002).

2   See Allen and Turner (2006) for a summary of research on the ethnic residential concentrations in U.S. metropolitan areas.

Chapter **6**

Comparing immigrant clustering patterns across metropolitan areas

This book began by posing several key research questions to focus the discussion and analysis of comparative urban development. These questions included the following: What spatial commonalities and differences exist in major metropolitan areas where immigrants are located? Where do immigrants settle in specific global metropolitan regions? Are there commonalities in immigrant clustering patterns in global cities? Are these patterns similar when analyzed at different scales? Having covered GIS methods to analyze these kinds of questions in part I (chapters 1 and 2) of this book, this chapter will now provide analysis results from three global metropolitan regions with significant immigrant population concentrations. These are the nine-county San Francisco Bay Area, New York metropolitan statistical area (MSA), and Los Angeles MSA.

At the core of the metropolitan areas selected for the analysis are global cities. Saskia Sassen in her book *The Global City* (1991), has described the global significance of New York, London, and Tokyo. Janet Abu-Lughod (1999) has studied the global cities of New York, Chicago, and Los Angeles. University of Loughborough's Globalization and World Cities Study Group and Network researchers in the United Kingdom *(www.lboro.ac.uk/gawc)* have developed a scoring system that uses firm data in accountancy, advertising, banking, and law to classify

Inventory of world cities	
Score	City
12	London, Paris, New York, Tokyo
10	Chicago, Frankfurt, Hong Kong, Los Angeles, Milan, Singapore
9	San Francisco, Sydney, Toronto, Zurich
8	Brussels, Madrid, Mexico City, São Paulo
7	Moscow, Seoul
6	Amsterdam, Boston, Caracas, Dallas, Dusseldorf, Geneva, Houston, Jakarta, Johannesburg, Melbourne, Osaka, Prague, Santiago, Taipei, Washington, D.C.
5	Bangkok, Beijing, Rome, Stockholm, Warsaw
4	Atlanta, Barcelona, Berlin, Buenos Aires, Budapest, Copenhagen, Hamburg, Istanbul, Kuala Lumpur, Manila, Miami, Minneapolis, Montreal, Munich, Shanghai

Table 6.1   The Globalization and World Cities Study Group and Network's inventory of world cities.

Source: GaWC data *(www.lboro.ac.uk/gawc)*.

and rank global cities in the world. London, Paris, New York, and Tokyo are all at the top of the hierarchy, as each has a score of 12 *(table 6.1)*.

Looking at the concentrations of immigrant populations using GIS maps of these global metropolitan regions, one can quickly see the clustering patterns. The analysis in this chapter, however, goes beyond just visually eyeballing patterns generated with GIS in thematic maps; it seeks to reveal any statistically significant differences in immigrant clustering patterns. By creating summary statistics for immigrant and nonimmigrant cluster areas and comparing these statistics across these groupings in three of the metropolitan regions located in the United States, we can see how GIS can be *loosely coupled* with standard statistical analysis to handle much more powerful analyses when compared to what each method of analysis can handle alone.[1] As in the previous chapter, the GIS and statistical analysis reported here is theory-driven. Specifically, this chapter discusses the extent to which households living in immigrant clusters of global metropolises are more likely to experience low homeownership rates, more overcrowding, and less assimilation when compared to the rest of the nonimmigrant areas in these regions. Exercise 5 on the CD shows how ArcGIS software can be used in creating variables with spatial information (contiguity) through a process of marking census tracts and classifying them as particular types of immigrant clusters.

One can analyze patterns in space with GIS at different scales. Map 6.1 shows the city and county of San Francisco as part of the nine-county San Francisco Bay Area. Chapter 5 discussed the spatial distribution of immigrants at the city/county level. The scope (scale) of analysis focused on the city/county level. The unit of analysis was the census tract. In the first part of this chapter we consider the following question: To what extent do the spatial patterns and statistically significant differences depicted at the city level discussed in chapter 5 hold true when analyzed at the metropolitan level? To empirically test this, we

Map 6.1   Scale of analysis: San Francisco in the San Francisco Bay Area.

Data sources: U.S. Census Bureau, Census 2000; Census 2000 TIGER/Line data down to the county level.

	San Francisco	Los Angeles	New York
China-born	4.0	1.5	1.7
Philippines-born	3.3	1.7	0.6
Mexico-born	6.6	14.6	1.1
Total population	7,039,362	16,373,645	21,199,865

Table 6.2   Levels of concentration for major immigrant groups by percent.

focus on three U.S. metropolitan regions with global significance for which uniform census data is available for the same foreign-born variables down to the census tract level: nine-county San Francisco Bay Area, Los Angeles MSA, and New York MSA. Table 6.2 shows the levels of concentration for major immigrant groups in the three regions. Immigrant clusters have been defined using these MSA figures and the same methodology described in chapter 5. For example, a China-born cluster in the Los Angeles MSA is comprised of spatially contiguous census tracts (5 percent above the MSA level—6.5 percent) and a core (10 percent above the MSA level—11.5 percent) *(figure 5.2)*.

Immigrant clusters in global metropolises in the United States

Using the cluster definition described above, the settlement patterns of China-born, Philippines-born, and Mexico-born groups in the three global metropolitan regions studied show a pattern of suburbanization of immigrant clusters. There are also interesting similarities and differences in housing market outcomes in these clusters as measured by homeownership rates, overcrowding, and assimilation indicators. The suburbanization of immigrant clusters is largely an overlooked phenomenon in the literature except in the context of limited-scope ethnographic studies that tell narratives about people living in such places as Monterey Park in the Los Angeles metropolitan region (Horton 1995). The suburbanized pattern of immigrant clusters in the three metropolitan regions is a new immigrant settlement pattern in comparison to what was typical during the earlier waves of immigration, when new arrivals were found entirely in inner city ethnic enclaves.

This chapter depicts spatial patterns by providing a cross-sectional snapshot of housing market outcomes across metropolitan areas in 2000, the most recent data available on the foreign-born population down to the census tract level. The analysis reveals significant distinctions among residential settlement patterns of different immigrant groups. One can also carry out temporal analysis to determine any changes in the number, location, and shape of immigrant clusters over time. This type of an analysis requires resolving any census tract boundary changes (e.g., due to splitting of large tracts) between 1990 and 2000 *(figure 2.1 in chapter 2)*.

	Native home-ownership rate	Immigrant home-ownership rate	Percent of metropolitan area's population that is foreign-born	Percent of total native-born U.S. population living in the metropolitan area	Percent of total immigrant population living in the metropolitan area
1980					
New York, NY	34	30.5	22	5.6	17.2
Los Angeles-Long Beach	53.9	39.4	19.4	4.6	12.0
San Francisco	56.3	54.4	13.8	2.3	4.0
1990					
New York, NY	37.9	31.5	25.6	4.3	13.6
Los Angeles-Long Beach	55.3	39.1	26.9	4.1	13.8
San Francisco	52.3	48.1	20.1	1.0	2.3
2000					
New York, NY	37.9	27.1	38.6	3.0	12.6
Los Angeles-Long Beach	56.5	37.5	41.6	2.7	12.8
San Francisco	49.8	39.2	26.6	0.8	1.9

Table 6.3   Metropolitan area differences in homeownership rates.

Source: Research Institute for Housing America 2002. "Homeownership in the Immigrant Population," George Borjas.

An important commonality among the immigrant groups in the United States is the way they function in very tight and expensive housing markets where even the native-born U.S. population has low homeownership rates. Table 6.3 shows homeownership rates for natives and immigrants in New York, Los Angeles–Long Beach, and San Francisco metropolitan areas. Notice that immigrant homeownership rates are consistently lower when compared to native homeownership rates in all of the three regions. For example, the homeownership rate for immigrant households in the Los Angeles–Long Beach metropolitan area in 2000 was only 37.5 percent. Homeownership rate for natives in 2000 stood at 56.5 percent, still far lower than the national average of 66.2 percent for all U.S. households.

Analysis reported in this chapter shows that across the three metropolitan areas, Mexico-born households live consistently in low homeownership clusters and are more likely to live in census tracts comprised predominantly of overcrowded dwellings. In contrast, China-born populations are mostly located in areas with high homeownership rates when compared to other groups. Income differences can partly account for the differences, but analyses at the household level by Painter et al. (2003) has found that after controlling for household mobility and other socioeconomic characteristics (including income), Chinese households still have homeownership rates 20 percentage points higher than their household characteristics would predict (Painter et al. 2003). It is clear that different immigrant groups face different types of challenges in global metropolitan housing markets that require a closer look. Spatial analysis with GIS provides a new perspective when analyzing such patterns.

Comparative analysis of immigrant clusters with 2000 census data

Comparative analyses of immigrant clusters in three major U.S. metropolitan regions with 2000 Census data largely fit the predictions of the spatial assimilation theory; but there are important variations, such as affluent China-born clusters in a central city setting in the case of San Francisco (discussed in chapter 5), and immigrant clusters in the suburbs. The following discussion reports analytical results focusing on three main outcome measures: homeownership, overcrowding, and assimilation indicators. Maps show the location of immigrant clusters in the three metropolitan regions. Tables compare selected housing and socioeconomic conditions inside and outside of immigrant clusters in each of the metropolitan regions for each of the three immigrant groups. Only statistically significant differences are reported in the following discussion.

China-born clusters

Spatial distribution of clusters. Maps 6.2, 6.3, and 6.4 show China-born clusters in the three metropolitan regions. A clear pattern shows the location of historic Chinatowns in central cities such as San Francisco and New York, and many other China-born clusters like Flushing, Sunset Park, and Elmhurst–Corona in the New York MSA; and Monterey Park–North San Gabriel Valley and Rowland Heights–South San Gabriel Valley concentrations in the Los Angeles MSA. Two of the largest China-born clusters in the Los Angeles MSA are in the suburbs.

Homeownership. In the Los Angeles MSA, China-born clusters are more likely to be occupied by homeowners (61.1 percent within China-born clusters compared to 52 percent outside of clusters) *(table 6.4)*. In contrast, the analysis for the nine-county San Francisco Bay Area shows that, on average, the percentage of units occupied by owners in China-born clusters (54.5 percent) is slightly (but statistically significantly) lower when compared to the rest of the Bay Area (58.9 percent). Similarly, in the New York MSA, China-born clusters are less likely to be occupied by homeowners (38.9 percent versus 52.2 percent). High rates of homeownership within China-born clusters in the New York MSA, however, are all at locations where median house values are relatively modest (under $300,000). New York's

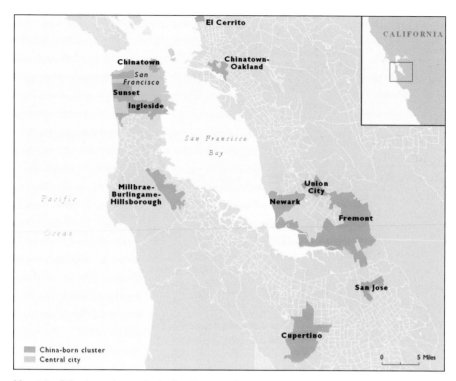

Map 6.2   China-born clusters in the San Francisco Bay Area, 2000.

Data sources: U.S. Census Bureau, Census 2000 Summary File 3 (SF 3), China-born population variable (PCT19034); Census 2000 TIGER/Line data down to the census tract level.

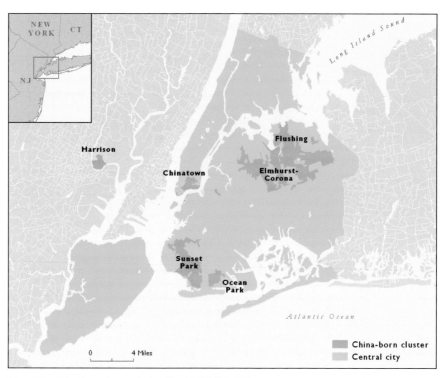

Map 6.3   China-born clusters in the New York MSA, 2000.

Data sources: U.S. Census Bureau, Census 2000 Summary File 3 (SF 3), China-born population variable (PCT19034); Census 2000 TIGER/Line data down to the census tract level.

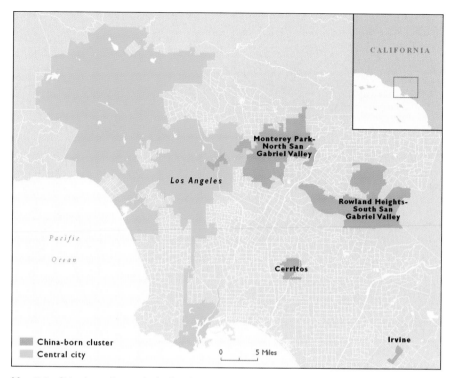

Map 6.4   China-born clusters in the Los Angeles MSA, 2000.

Data sources: U.S. Census Bureau, Census 2000 Summary File 3 (SF 3), China-born population variable (PCT19034); Census 2000 TIGER/Line data down to the census tract level.

San Francisco Bay Area		
Ethnic group and characteristics	Within China-born clusters	Outside of China-born clusters
China-born clusters		
Mean percent overcrowded		
owner occupied, more than 1 occupant per room	12.5**	7.6**
renter occupied, more than 1 occupant per room	19.6**	16.7**
Mean percent cost burdened		
(>50 percent of income spent on rent)	16.2**	17.4**
Mean percent homeownership	54.5**	58.9**
Mean percent without kitchen	2.4**	1.0**
Mean percent in poverty	16.5	15.5
Mean percent year of entry		
1990 to March 2000	39.3**	37.0**
1965 to 1989	51.7	50.2
Mean percent resided in a foreign country, 1995	9.1**	5.2**
Mean percent linguistically isolated		
Asian-speaking households	14**	3.1**

Los Angeles MSA		
Ethnic group and characteristics	Within China-born clusters	Outside of China-born clusters
China-born clusters		
Mean percent overcrowded		
owner occupied, more than 1 occupant per room	14.0	17.6
renter occupied, more than 1 occupant per room	28.1	30.0
Mean percent cost burdened		
(>50 percent of income spent on rent)	20.4	20.3
Mean percent homeownership	61.1**	52.0**
Mean percent without kitchen	1.4	1.7
Mean percent in poverty	15.0**	23.5**
Mean percent year of entry		
1990 to March 2000	33.7	31.7
1965 to 1989	59.3	58.6
Mean percent resided in a foreign country, 1995	7.4**	4.9**
Mean percent linguistically isolated		
Asian-speaking households	17.5**	2.7**
New York MSA		
Ethnic group and characteristics	Within China-born clusters	Outside of China-born clusters
China-born clusters		
Mean percent overcrowded		
owner occupied, more than 1 occupant per room	12.8**	5.8**
renter occupied, more than 1 occupant per room	22.6**	12.4**
Mean percent cost burdened		
(>50 percent of income spent on rent)	23.1**	20.1**
Mean percent homeownership	38.9**	52.2**
Mean percent without kitchen	1.2	1.0
Mean percent in poverty	25.7**	21.6**
Mean percent year of entry		
1990 to March 2000	44.5**	35.2**
1965 to 1989	46.5**	49.2**
Mean percent resided in a foreign country, 1995	9.9**	4.6**
Mean percent linguistically isolated		
Asian-speaking households	12.1**	1.0**

$*p < .10$, $**p < .05$ (two-tail test)

Note: There are three types of immigrant clusters: China-Born clusters, Philippines-born clusters, and Mexico-born clusters. The clusters are defined as a set of contiguous tracts that contain at least one tract where a group is represented at a rate 10 percentage points above the group's share in the total population and whose other tracts each have an immigrant concentration level of at least 5 percentage points above the group's share in the total population in the respective regions.

Table 6.4   China-born cluster areas in three MSAs.

Chinatown in the central city resembles the zones-in-transition type of neighborhood with low percentages of homeownership and low incomes.

Overcrowding. In the nine-county San Francisco Bay Area, dwelling units in China-born clusters are more likely to be overcrowded when compared to units in the non-China-born cluster areas throughout the region. On average, 12.5 percent of the dwelling units occupied by owners in the San Francisco Bay Area's China-born clusters are overcrowded (more than one person per room) when compared with units occupied by owners in the rest of the region (7.6 percent). This suggests that homeownership in areas where the China-born are concentrated involves extended families and that homeowners in the China-born clusters are more likely to live in housing conditions that are considered overcrowded.

Similarly, in the New York MSA, China-born clusters are more likely to have overcrowding for owners and renters (12.8 percent versus 5.8 percent, and 22.6 percent and 12.4 percent, respectively). In contrast, in the Los Angeles MSA the differences in overcrowding inside and outside of China-born clusters are statistically insignificant.

Assimilation indicators. In the San Francisco Bay Area, China-born clusters are more likely to be populated by households who are linguistically isolated when compared to the rest of the region (14 percent versus 3.1 percent). The same pattern holds true in the Los Angeles MSA (17.5 percent versus 2.7 percent) and in the New York MSA (12.1 percent versus 1 percent). The finding of linguistic isolation and recent immigrants in suburban immigrant clusters is unexpected under the spatial assimilation theory. In the San Francisco Bay Area and New York MSA, China-born clusters are more likely to be populated by recent immigrants who have entered the United States between 1990 and 2000.

Philippines-born clustering patterns

Spatial distribution of clusters. Maps 6.5, 6.6, and 6.7 show Philippines-born clusters in the three metropolitan regions. In the New York MSA, Philippines-born clusters are located in Elmhurst-Maspeth, Hillcrest-Fresh Meadows, and Jersey City. Some of these clusters are in neighborhoods with large hospitals. Thirty percent of Filipinos in the city and its suburbs work as nurses or other health practitioners (*The New York Times* 2003).

Homeownership. San Francisco Bay Area's Philippines-born clusters include areas in Daly City, South of Market neighborhood in San Francisco, Vallejo, Alameda, Pleasant Hill, Hercules, San Jose, Santa Clara, Martinez, Hayward, and Milpitas. Housing units located in these clusters are more likely to be occupied by owners *(table 6.5)*. On average, 64.9 percent of the units within a Philippines-born cluster are occupied by owners, compared with 57.8 percent in the rest of the nine-county San Francisco Bay Area. Like in the China-born clusters, Filipinos seem to express a preference for homeownership where other Filipinos

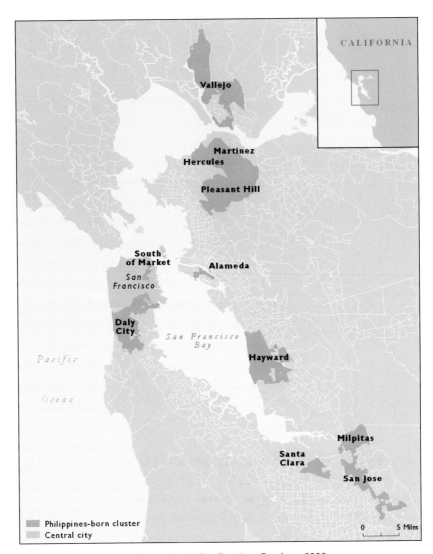

Map 6.5 Philippines-born clusters in the San Francisco Bay Area, 2000.

Data sources: U.S. Census Bureau, Census 2000 Summary File 3 (SF 3), Philippines-born population variable (PCT19053); Census 2000 TIGER/Line data down to the census tract level.

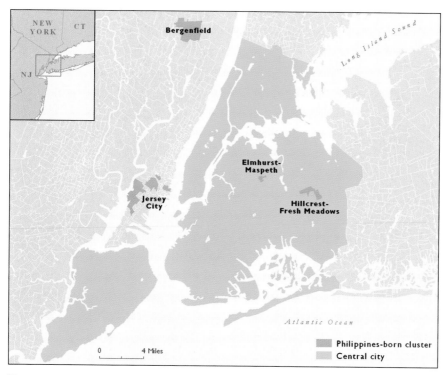

Map 6.6   Philippines-born clusters in the New York MSA, 2000.

Data sources: U.S. Census Bureau, Census 2000 Summary File 3 (SF 3), Philippines-born population variable (PCT19053); Census 2000 TIGER/Line data down to the census tract level.

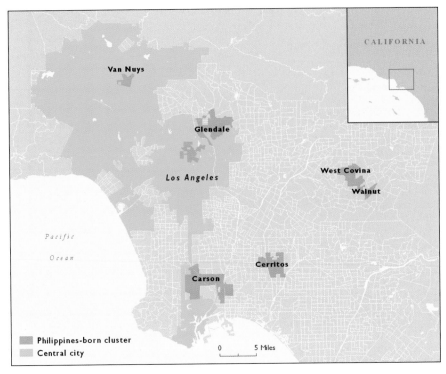

Map 6.7   Philippines-born clusters in the Los Angeles MSA, 2000.

Data sources: U.S. Census Bureau, Census 2000 Summary File 3 (SF 3), Philippines-born population variable (PCT19053); Census 2000 TIGER/Line data down to the census tract level.

are concentrated. In New York, Logan et al. (2002) has also found that, based on analysis of 1990 Census data, the more affluent Filipinos are more likely to live in an ethnic cluster and enjoy homeownership. In the San Francisco Bay Area, high homeownership rates are found in the suburbs of San Francisco (e.g., Daly City), the northern portions of the San Francisco Bay, and in the suburbs of San Jose. Homeownership is pronounced in modestly priced ($300,000–$500,000) parts of the Philippines-born clusters. New York MSA's Philippines-born clusters are located in the suburbs with modest home prices (less than $300,000). Several distinct clusters of the Philippines-born population are located in the suburbs where homeownership rates are high and where house values are relatively modest (less than $300,000). Philippines-born clusters in the three regions are predominantly in suburban locations.

Overcrowding. In the San Francisco Bay Area, units within the Philippines-born clusters are more likely to be overcrowded both for renters (29.3 percent within clusters when compared to 15.7 percent outside of clusters) and for owners (17 percent versus 7.2 percent). Likewise, in the New York MSA, units within the Philippines-born clusters are more likely

San Francisco Bay Area		
Ethnic group and characteristics	Within Philippines-born clusters	Outside of Philippines-born clusters
Philippines-born clusters		
Mean percent overcrowded		
owner occupied, more than 1 occupant per room	17.0**	7.2**
renter occupied, more than 1 occupant per room	29.3**	15.7**
Mean percent cost burdened		
(>50 percent of income spent on rent)	17.8	17.3
Mean percent homeownership	64.9**	57.8**
Mean percent without kitchen	1.5	1.1
Mean percent in poverty	11.8	16.0
Mean percent year of entry		
1990 to March 2000	34.8**	37.5**
1990 to March 2000	58.5**	49.5**
Mean percent resided in a foreign country, 1995	6.1	5.6
Mean percent linguistically isolated		
Asian-speaking households	9.1**	3.7**

Los Angeles, MSA		
Ethnic group and characteristics	Within Philippines-born clusters	Outside of Philippines-born clusters
Philippines-born clusters		
Mean percent overcrowded		
owner occupied, more than 1 occupant per room	21.8**	17.2**
renter occupied, more than 1 occupant per room	36.8	29.5
Mean percent cost burdened		
(>50 percent of income spent on rent)	20.4	20.3
Mean percent homeownership	48.6	52.7
Mean percent without kitchen	1.7	1.7
Mean percent in poverty	20.4	23.1
Mean percent year of entry		
1990 to March 2000	32.6	31.8
1965 to 1989	61.5**	58.5**
Mean percent resided in a foreign country, 1995	6.2**	5.0**
Mean percent linguistically isolated		
Asian-speaking households	6.6**	3.5**

New York MSA		
Ethnic group and characteristics	Within Philippines-born clusters	Outside of Philippines-born clusters
Philippines-born clusters		
Mean percent overcrowded		
owner occupied, more than 1 occupant per room	9.4**	6.2**
renter occupied, more than 1 occupant per room	17.5**	13.0**
Mean percent cost burdened		
(>50 percent of income spent on rent)	18.3	20.3
Mean percent homeownership	46.1	51.5
Mean percent without kitchen	1.1	1.1
Mean percent in poverty	19.2	21.9
Mean percent year of entry		
1990 to March 2000	43.6**	35.7**
1965 to 1989	49.8	49.1
Mean percent resided in a foreign country, 1995	7.9**	4.9**
Mean percent linguistically isolated		
Asian-speaking households	4.9**	1.6**
**p < .05 (two-tail test)		
Note: There are three types of immigrant clusters: China-born clusters, Philippines-born clusters, and Mexico-born clusters. The clusters are defined as a set of contiguous tracts, that contain at least one tract where a group is represented at a rate 10 percentage points above the group's share in the total population and whose other tracts each have an immigrant concentration level of at least 5 percentage points above the group's share in the total population in the respective regions.		

Table 6.5   Philippines-born cluster areas in three MSAs.

to be overcrowded both for renters (17.5 percent versus 13 percent) and for owners (9.4 percent versus 6.2 percent). In the Los Angeles MSA, units within the Philippines-born clusters are more likely to be overcrowded for owners only (21.8 percent versus 17.2 percent).

Assimilation indicators. In all three MSAs, households in Philippines-born clusters are more likely to experience linguistic isolation. In the Los Angeles MSA, Philippines-born clusters are more likely to be populated by relatively established immigrants (when compared to the rest of the region) who have entered the United States between 1965 and 1989. In the New York MSA, Philippines-born clusters are more likely to be populated by recent immigrants who have entered the United States between 1990 and 2000. In the San Francisco Bay Area, differences in terms of year of entry between the clusters and the rest of the region are statistically significant for both recent and more established immigrants, indicating a mix in the Philippines-born clusters.

Mexico-born clustering patterns

Spatial distribution of clusters. Maps 6.8, 6.9, and 6.10 show Mexico-born clusters in the three metropolitan regions, revealing the prevalence of Mexico-born populations in outlying rural areas of the three metropolitan regions as well as concentrations in central city locations.

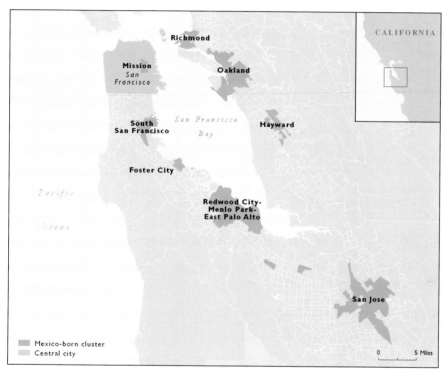

Map 6.8   Mexico-born clusters in the San Francisco Bay Area, 2000.

Data sources: U.S. Census Bureau, Census 2000 Summary File 3 (SF 3), Mexico-born population variable (PCT19103); Census 2000 TIGER/Line data down to the census tract level.

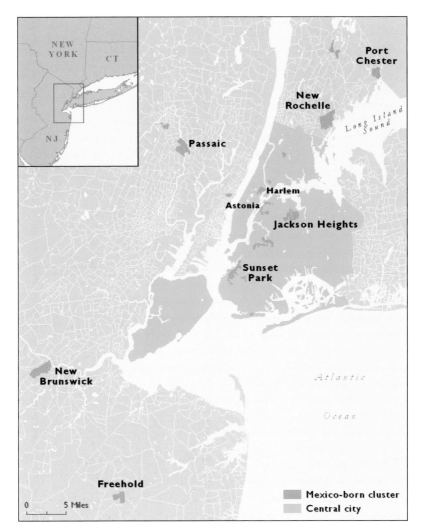

Map 6.9 Mexico-born clusters in the New York MSA, 2000.

Data sources: U.S. Census Bureau, Census 2000 Summary File 3 (SF 3), Mexico-born population variable (PCT19103); Census 2000 TIGER/Line data down to the census tract level.

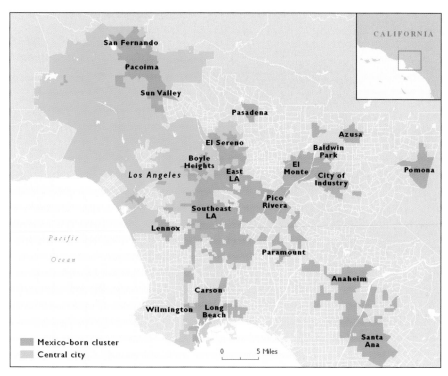

Map 6.10   Mexico-born clusters in the Los Angeles MSA, 2000.

Data sources: U.S. Census Bureau, Census 2000 Summary File 3 (SF 3), Mexico-born population variable (PCT19103); Census 2000 TIGER/Line data down to the census tract level.

Homeownership. Unlike the China-born and the Philippines-born clusters discussed above, homeownership is less prevalent within Mexico-born clusters *(table 6.6)*. In the San Francisco Bay Area, on average, 44.6 percent of units are occupied by owners within Mexico-born clusters, compared with 60 percent in the rest of the MSA. These findings are consistent with the spatial assimilation theory predicting that, in general, immigrants who are economically better off are found outside of ethnic clusters. Mexico-born clusters in particular do not seem to retain immigrants who improve their economic conditions over time. In the New York MSA, units within the Mexico-born clusters are less likely to be homeowners (21.1 percent versus 52.3 percent). Similarly, in the Los Angeles MSA, units within the Mexico-born clusters are less likely to be homeowners (39.8 percent versus 57.3 percent). In the Los Angeles MSA, Mexico-born households have a major presence in census tracts where house values are less than $300,000.

Overcrowding. Overall, both owner-occupied and renter-occupied dwelling units in Mexico-born clusters are more likely to be overcrowded. This is true for the San Francisco Bay Area (23.5 percent versus 6.1 percent for owners, and 39.3 percent versus 14.2 percent for

San Francisco Bay Area		
Ethnic group and characteristics	Within Mexico-born clusters	Outside of Mexico-born clusters
Mexico-born clusters		
Mean percent overcrowded		
owner occupied, more than 1 occupant per room	23.5**	6.1**
renter occupied, more than 1 occupant per room	39.3**	14.2**
Mean percent cost burdened		
(>50 percent of income spent on rent)	20.8**	16.9**
Mean percent homeownership	44.6**	60.0**
Mean percent without kitchen	1.4	1.1
Mean percent in poverty	19.6	15.2
Mean percent year of entry		
1990 to March 2000	47.4**	36.0**
1965 to 1989	48.0**	50.6**
Mean percent resided in a foreign country, 1995	8.2**	5.3**
Mean percent linguistically isolated		
Spanish-speaking households	11.2**	2.1**
Los Angeles MSA		
Ethnic group and characteristics	Within Mexico-born clusters	Outside of Mexico-born clusters
Mexico-born clusters		
Mean percent overcrowded		
owner occupied, more than 1 occupant per room	36.4**	10.2**
renter occupied, more than 1 occupant per room	53.7**	20.7**
Mean percent cost burdened		
(>50 percent of income spent on rent)	22.5**	19.4**
Mean percent homeownership	39.8**	57.3**
Mean percent without kitchen	2.5**	1.4**
Mean percent in poverty	30.1**	20.3**
Mean percent year of entry		
1990 to March 2000	36.7**	30.0**
1965 to 1989	58.9	58.5
Mean percent resided in a foreign country, 1995	6.7	4.4
Mean percent linguistically isolated		
Spanish-speaking households	23.7**	5.4**

New York MSA		
Ethnic group and characteristics	Within Mexico-born clusters	Outside of Mexico-born clusters
Mexico-born clusters		
Mean percent overcrowded		
owner occupied, more than 1 occupant per room	14.2**	6.0**
renter occupied, more than 1 occupant per room	29.8**	12.5**
Mean percent cost burdened		
(>50 percent of income spent on rent)	24.6**	20.1**
Mean percent homeownership	21.1**	52.3**
Mean percent without kitchen	2.1**	1.0**
Mean percent in poverty	36.2**	21.4**
Mean percent year of entry		
1990 to March 2000	54.7**	35.2**
1965 to 1989	41.3**	49.3**
Mean percent resided in a foreign country, 1995	10.7**	4.7**
Mean percent linguistically isolated		
Spanish-speaking households	22.2**	4.7**
**p < .05 (two-tail test)		
Note: There are three types of immigrant clusters: China-born clusters, Philippines-born clusters, and Mexico-born clusters. The clusters are defined as a set of contiguous tracts that contain at least one tract where a group is represented at a rate 10 percentage points above the group's share in the total population and whose other tracts each have an immigrant concentration level of at least 5 percentage points above the group's share in the total population in the respective regions.		

Table 6.6 Mexico-born cluster areas in three MSAs.

Data sources: U.S. Census Bureau, Census 2000 Summary File 3 (SF3), Mexico-born population variable (PCT 19103); Census 2000 TIGER/Line data down to the census tract level.

renters), the Los Angeles MSA (53.7 percent versus 20.7 percent for renters, 36.4 percent versus 10.2 percent for owners), and the New York MSA (29.8 percent versus 12.5 percent for renters, 14.2 percent versus 6 percent for owners).

Assimilation indicators. Overall, Mexico-born clusters display characteristics that fit the zones-in-transition model better than either the Philippines-born or the China-born clusters. A significant percentage of the foreign-born population living in Mexico-born clusters in the San Francisco Bay Area is recent immigrants who have entered the United States between 1990 and 2000 (47.4 percent), compared to others in the rest of the MSA (36 percent). In the New York MSA, units within the Mexico-born clusters are more likely to have entered between 1990 and 2000 (54.7 percent versus 35.2 percent). A similar trend is seen in the Los Angeles MSA (36.7 percent versus 30 percent).

The analysis above shows some common patterns in the way different immigrant groups have settled in the three metropolitan regions. The finding of major suburban clusters of China-born and Philippines-born immigrants in all of the three metropolitan regions shows a clear pattern of suburbanization for these groups. Many have realized homeownership in suburban immigrant clusters comprised of modestly priced homes. The Mexico-born population, on the other hand, is experiencing significant housing-related problems such as overcrowding and high costs of housing in all of the three regions. In the Los Angeles MSA, the Mexico-born population is pronounced in areas of affordable rental housing. In the San Francisco Bay Area, a distinct cluster is found in San Francisco's relatively lower-income Mission District (as discussed in chapter 5), and in pockets of rural areas throughout the region.

In summary, as discussed in this chapter, immigrant clustering patterns can be spatially analyzed using GIS, and additional statistical analyses can be carried out using a statistical software package like SPSS, STATA, or SAS. Access to high-quality spatial data, however, remains as a significant barrier for researchers wanting to carry out empirical and spatial analysis to understand comparative urban development. The uniform and easy-to-access format of U.S. Census data makes quantitative analysis for U.S. cities relatively easy. Replicating similar studies in other countries becomes difficult because of limited availability of census data on the Internet, language barriers, and varying standards in how census variables are defined and reported. Cross-national census data analysis using GIS is still in its infancy. Efforts to standardize spatial data and to make it widely available on the Internet (as discussed in chapter 2) are likely to make such analyses far easier in the future. Until then, as had been done in this book, analysis of human settlements using international census data requires piecing together hard-to-find data with care.

Conclusion and future research directions

The type of detailed census data analysis covered in part III of this book, focusing on metropolitan areas with global significance in the United States, can be replicated (with variables defined slightly differently) in other regions of the world where census data collection and reporting activities are highly developed, such as in European Union countries. Following the same theoretical interest in understanding immigrant settlement patterns, at this point we are faced with two main challenges: (1) to what extent is it appropriate to analyze urban development patterns from the lens of the American urban development experience? and (2) how do we deal with various methods and definitions used in the research literature on European immigrant clustering patterns that complicates cross-national analysis? After all, context matters, and the analysis of spatial data needs to be grounded with the urban development experiences and histories of particular places, as was done in chapter 5 of this book in the case of San Francisco.

Because internationally comparable data on the spatial patterns of immigrant populations and their housing conditions are not readily available, we have to rely on the research literature on understanding immigrant settlement patterns in Europe. Patrick Le Gales (2002), in his book *European Cities*, cautions us against making generalizations and statements about European cities solely based on the experience of American cities. There are indeed important differences in how American and European cities have developed, in residential location decisions of households, and in how housing markets work. An important difference is that the social safety net in Europe for low-income households is much stronger. The social housing sector has historically been an important aspect of the housing delivery system in much of Europe under social welfare governments. At the time of this writing, European cities are facing new challenges, including changing demographics of Europe (aging native population), increasing presence of immigrants from other European countries and the developing world, the influence of globalization, and new institutional arrangements and requirements set by the European Union regulating most aspects of economic and social life. Among others, the better integration of immigrants into cities has now become an important social policy issue in Europe (Rifkin 2004).

Following the same thread of research interests, we can ask the following: To what extent do large cities with global significance in Europe (like Paris and Amsterdam) show similar dynamics as in other global cities like San Francisco? As discussed in chapter 1 of this book, the Paris metropolitan region has received significant numbers of immigrants—from Morocco and Turkey. Spatial analysis of immigrant concentrations (all groups) showed clusters in the northern suburbs of Paris *(chapter 1, map 1.4)*. In Amsterdam, the largest concentrations of immigrants come from Suriname, Morocco, and Turkey. Based on their analysis of immigrant clusters between 1994 and 1999 in Amsterdam (using post codes as their unit of analysis), Musterd and Deurloo (2002) concluded that immigrant clustering patterns were significantly shaped by the availability of affordable social housing stock in certain areas of Dutch cities. A similar dynamic was at work in Paris where immigrants are concentrated in areas where large blocks of land have been built by the French government known as HLM (*habitations à loyer modéré*—low-rent dwellings) as discussed in chapter 1. Likewise, in Sweden a disproportionate number of immigrants live in the least desirable housing stock in its middle-sized municipalities. Fieldwork research planned in Paris, Amsterdam, Stockholm, and Istanbul for the next phase of this project will analyze housing markets and the spatial analysis of immigrant settlement patterns with GIS.

We have covered a lot of ground in this book. Part I introduced fundamental spatial analysis concepts and sources of spatial data to carry out spatial analysis with GIS. Part II provided exemplary uses of GIS in local government and nonprofit settings throughout the world and the use of GIS in solving public policy problems for social service delivery agencies. Part III of the book focused on theories of immigrant settlement patterns in global cities and demonstrated the use of census data in spatial analysis.

Now, I invite you to work through the exercises on the CD that use some of the same data analyzed and displayed on the maps.

Notes

1   For a review of descriptive and inferential statistics, see the following widely used and excellent textbooks: *Statistics: A Tool for Social Research*, seventh edition, by Joseph F. Healey (2005), and *Social Statistics for a Diverse Society*, fourth edition, by Chava Frankfort-Nachmias and Anna Leon-Guerrero (2006).

References and additional resources

Abu-Lughod, Janet L. 1999. *New York, Chicago, Los Angeles: America's global cities.* Minneapolis: University of Minnesota Press.

Alba, Richard D., John R. Logan, Brian. J. Stults, Gilbert Marzan, and Wenquan Zhang. 1999. Immigrant groups in the suburbs: A reexamination of suburbanization and spatial assimilation. *American Sociological Review* 64:446–60.

Alba, Richard D., John R. Logan, and Kyle Crowder. 1997. White ethnic neighborhoods and assimilation: The greater New York region, 1980–1990. *Social Forces.* 75(3): 883–909.

Alba, Richard D., and Victor Nee. 2003. *Remaking the American mainstream: Assimilation and contemporary immigration.* Cambridge, Mass.: Harvard University Press.

Allen, James P., and Eugene Turner. 1996. Spatial patterns of immigrant assimilation. *Professional Geographer.* 48(2): 140–55.

———. April 2006. Ethnic residential concentrations in United States metropolitan areas. *The Geographical Review* 95(2): 267–85.

Angel, Shlomo. 2000. *Housing policy matters: A global analysis.* New York: Oxford University Press.

Babbie, Earl. 2001. *The practice of social research.* 9th ed. Belmont, Calif.: Wadsworth/Thomson Learning.

———. 2004. *The practice of social research.* 10th ed. Belmont, Calif.: Wadsworth/Thomson Learning.

Bailey, Trevor C., and Anthony C. Gatrell. 1995. *Interactive spatial data analysis.* New York, N.Y.: John Wiley and Sons, Inc.

Bardach, Eugene. 2005. *A practical guide for policy analysis: The eightfold path to more effective problem solving.* 2nd ed. Washington, D.C.: CQ press.

Barnett, W. Steven, and Sarane S. Boocock. 1998. *Early care and education for children in poverty: Promises, programs, and long-term results.* Albany, N.Y.: State University of New York Press.

Beaverstock, J. V., R. G. Smith, P. J. Taylor, D. R. F. Walker, and H. Lorimer. 2000. Globalization and world cities: Some measurement methodologies. *Applied Geography* 20(1): 43–63.

Beveridge, Andrew A. 2002. Immigration, ethnicity, and race in metropolitan New York, 1990–2000. In *Past time, past place: GIS for history*, ed. Anne Kelly Knowles. Redlands, Calif.: ESRI Press.

Borjas, George J. 2002. Homeownership in the immigrant population. Faculty Working Paper 02–01, Research Institute for Housing America. Washington, D.C.

Bost, Kelly K., K. L. Cielinski, Wanda H. Newell, and Brian E. Vaughn. 1994. Social networks of children attending Head Start from the perspective of the child. *Early Childhood Research Quarterly* 9:441–62.

Brail, Richard K., and Richard E. Klosterman, eds. 2001. *Planning support systems: Integrating geographic information systems, models, and visualization tools.* Redlands, Calif: ESRI Press.

Brenner, Neil, and Roger Keil. 2006. *The global cities reader.* London: Routledge.

Brewer, Cynthia A. 2005. *Designing better maps: A guide for GIS users.* Redlands, Calif.: ESRI Press.

Briggs, Xavier de Souza, ed. 2005. *The geography of opportunity: Race and housing choice in metropolitan America.* Washington, D.C.: Brookings Institution Press.

Brooks-Gunn, Jeanne, Greg J. Duncan, Pamela Kato Klebanov, and Naomi Sealand. 1993. Do neighborhoods influence child and adolescent development? *American Journal of Sociology* 99(2): 353–95.

Budic, Zorica D. 1994. Effectiveness of geographic information systems in local planning. *Journal of American Planning Association* 60(2): 244–63.

Burgess, Ernest W. 1925. The growth of the city: An introduction to a research project. In *The city*, ed. Robert Park, Ernest W. Burgess, R. D. McKenzie. Chicago: The University of Chicago Press.

Can, Ayse. 1998. GIS and spatial analysis of housing and mortgage markets. *Journal of Housing Research* 9(1): 61–86.

Castells, Manuel. 1983. Urban poverty, ethnic minorities and community organization: The experience of neighborhood mobilization in San Francisco's Mission District In *The city and the grassroots*, 106–37. Berkeley: University of California Press.

———. 2000. *The rise of the network society.* 2nd ed. Oxford, U.K.: Blackwell Publishers.

Clark, David. 2003. *Urban world/global city.* 2nd ed. London: Routledge.

Clarke, Keith C. 2003. *Getting started with geographic information systems.* 4th ed. Upper Saddle River, N.J.: Prentice Hall.

———. August 4, 2005. Lecture at Spatially Integrated Social Science (SPACE) Workshop. San Francisco: San Francisco State University.

Clarke-Stewart, Alison, and Virginia D. Allhusen. 2005. *What we know about childcare.* Cambridge, Mass.: Harvard University Press.

Craig, William J., Trevor M. Harris, and Daniel Weiner, eds. 2002. *Community participation and geographic information systems.* London: Taylor and Francis.

Currie, Janet. 2001. Early childhood education programs. *Journal of Economic Perspective* 15(2): 213–38.

Dandekar, Hemalata C., ed. 2003. *The planner's use of information.* 2nd ed. Chicago, Ill.: Planners Press, American Planning Association.

Davis, Diane. E. 2005. Cities in global context: A brief intellectual history. *International Journal of Urban and Regional Research.* 29(1): 92–109.

DeLeon, Richard E. 1992. *Left coast city: Progressive politics in San Francisco: 1975–1991.* Lawrence, Kans.: University Press of Kansas.

Demers, Michael N. 2005. *Fundamentals of geographic information systems.* Hoboken, N.J.: John Wiley and Sons, Inc.

Dent, Borden D. 1999. *Cartography: Thematic map design.* 5th ed. Boston, Mass.: WCB/McGraw Hill.

Dowall, David E. 1995. The land market assessment: A new tool for urban management. Urban Management Programme Tool No. 4. Washington, D.C.: World Bank.

Deurloo, Marinus C., and Sako Musterd. 1998. Ethnic clusters in Amsterdam, 1994–96: A micro-area analysis. *Urban Studies* 35(3): 385–96.

Duncan, Greg J. and Stephen W. Raudenbush. 1999. Assessing the effects of context in studies of child and youth development. *Educational Psychologist* 34(1): 29–41.

Elwood, Sarah, and Helga Leitner. 2003. GIS and spatial knowledge production for neighborhood revitalization: Negotiating state priorities and neighborhood visions. *Journal of Urban Affairs* 25(2): 139–57.

Fainstein, Susan S. 2002. Inequality in global city-regions. In *Global city-regions: Trends, theory, policy*, ed Allen J. Scott, 285–98. New York: Oxford University Press.

Fix, Michael, and Jeffrey S. Passel. May 1994. Immigration and immigrants: Setting the record straight. Washington, D.C.: The Urban Institute.

Flood, Joe. 1997. Urban and housing indicators. *Urban Studies* 34(10): 1635–65.

Florida, Richard. 2002. *The rise of the creative class and how it's transforming work, leisure, community, and everyday life.* New York: Basic Books.

Fotheringham, A. Stewart, and Michael Wegener, eds. 2000. *Spatial models and GIS: New potential and new models.* London: Taylor and Francis.

Frankfort-Nachmias, Chava, and A. Leon-Guerrero. 2006. *Social statistics for a diverse society.* 4th ed. Thousand Oaks, Calif.: Pine Forge Press.

French, S. P., and L. L. Wiggins. 1990. California planning agency experiences with automated mapping and geographic information systems. *Environment and Planning B* 17(4): 441–50.

Friedmann, John. 1987. Planning in the public domain: From knowledge to action. Princeton, N.J.: Princeton University Press.

Friedmann, John, and Goetz Wolff. 1982. World city formation: An agenda for research and action. *International Journal of Urban and Regional Research* 6: 309–44.

Galster, G. C., and M. Mikelsons. 1995. The geography of metropolitan opportunity: A case study of neighborhood conditions confronting youth in Washington, D.C. *Housing Policy Debate* 6(1): 73–102.

Galster, G. C., and Sean P. Killen. 1995. The geography of metropolitan opportunity: A reconnaissance and conceptual framework. *Housing Policy Debate* 6(1): 7–43.

Gaubert, Patrice, Smail Ibbou, and Christian Tutin. 1996. Segmented real estate markets and price mechanisms: The case of Paris. *International Journal of Urban and Regional Research,* 270–98.

Godfrey, Brian J. 1988. *Neighborhoods in transition: The making of San Francisco's ethnic and nonconformist communities.* Berkeley: University of California Press.

———. July 1997. Urban development and redevelopment in San Francisco. *Geographical Review.* 87(3).

Goodchild, Michael F., and Donald G. Janelle, eds. 2004. *Spatially integrated social science.* New York: Oxford University Press.

Graham, Stephen. 1999. Global grids of glass: On global cities, telecommunications, and planetary urban networks. *Urban Studies* 36 (5/6): 929–49.

———. 2002. Bridging urban digital divides? Urban polarisation and information and communications technologies (ICTs) *Urban Studies* 39(1): 33–56.

Gray, Robert, and Barbara Haley. September 25, 2003. Assisted Housing Data. Presentation at the Housing Statistics Users Group (HSUG-West) Conference, Berkeley Program on Housing and Urban Policy. Berkeley: University of California, Berkeley. urbanpolicy.berkeley.edu/hsugwest.htm.

Greene, Richard W. 2000. *GIS in public policy: Using geographic information for more effective government.* Redlands, Calif: ESRI Press.

Haithcoat, Timothy, Lisa Warnecke, and Zorica Nedovic-Budic. 2001. Geographic information technology in local government: Experience and issues. In *The municipal year book 2001*, 47–57. Washington, D.C.: International City/County Management Association (ICMA).

Hall, Peter. 1966. *The world cities.* New York: McGraw-Hill.

———. 1977. *The world cities.* 2nd ed. London: Weidenfeld and Nicolson.

———. 2002. Global city-regions in the twenty-first century. In *Global city-regions: Trends, theory, policy*, ed. Allen J. Scott, 59–77. New York: Oxford University Press.

Harris, Britton, and Michael Batty. 2001. Locational models, geographic information, and planning support systems. In *Planning support systems: Integrating geographic information systems, models, and visualization tools*, ed. Richard K. Brail and Richard E. Klosterman, 25–57 Redlands, Calif.: ESRI Press.

Hartman, Chester. 2002. *City for sale: The transformation of San Francisco.* Berkeley: University of California Press.

Harwood, Stacy, and Dowell Myers. 2002. The dynamics of immigration and local governance in Santa Ana: Neighborhood activism, overcrowding, and land-use policy. *Policy Studies Journal* 30(1): 70–91.

Healey, Joseph F. 2002. *Statistics: A tool for social research.* 6th ed. Belmont, Calif.: Wadsworth/Thomson Learning.

———. 2005. *Statistics: A tool for social research.* 7th ed. Belmont, Calif.: Wadsworth/ Thomson Learning.

Hill, M. S., and J. R. Sandfort. 1995. Effects of childhood poverty on productivity later in life: Implications for public policy. *Children and Youth Services Review* 17(1/2): 91–126.

Hillier, A. E. 2003. Spatial analysis of historical redlining: A methodological exploration. *Journal of Housing Research* 14(1): 137–67.

Hofferth, S. L. 1994. Who enrolls in Head Start? A demographic analysis of Head Start-eligible children. *Early Childhood Research Quarterly.* 9:243–68.

Hopkins, Lew, Faranak Miraftab, Zorica Nedovic-Budic, and Emily Talen. February 2002. An analysis of urban indicators using geographic information science. Report prepared for U.S. Department of Housing and Urban Development and UCGIS.

Horton, John. 1995. *The politics of diversity: Immigration, resistance, and change in Monterey Park, California.* Philadelphia: Temple University Press.

Hum, Tarry. 2002. Asian and Latino immigration and the revitalization of Sunset Park, Brooklyn. In *Contemporary Asian American communities: Intersections and divergences,* ed. Linda Trinh Vo and Rick Bonus. Philadelphia: Temple University Press.

Huston, A. C., V. C. McLoyd, C. G. Coll. 1994. Children in poverty: Issues in contemporary research. *Child Development* 65:275–82.

Innes, Judith E. 1990. *Knowledge and public policy: The search for meaningful indicators.* New Brunswick, N.J.: Transaction Publishers.

Innes, Judith.E., and David M. Simpson. 1993. Implementing GIS for planning: Lessons from the history of technological innovation. *Journal of American Planning Association.* 59(2): 230–36.

Jargowski, Paul A. 1997. *Poverty and place: Ghettos, barrios and the American city.* New York: Russell Sage Foundation.

Joint Center for Housing Studies of Harvard University. 2005. *The state of the nation's housing.* Cambridge, Mass.: Harvard College. www.jchs.harvard.edu

Kalita, S. Mitra. 2003. *Suburban Sahibs: Three immigrant families and their passage from India to America.* New Brunswick, N.J.: Rutgers University Press.

Kasarda, J. D. 1993. Inner-city concentrated poverty and neighborhood distress: 1970 to 1990. *Housing Policy Debate* 4(3): 253–302.

Keyder, Caglar. 2005. Globalization and social exclusion in Istanbul. *International Journal of Urban and Regional Research.* 29(1): 124–34.

Klosterman, Richard. 2001. Planning support systems: A new perspective on computer-aided planning. In *Planning support systems: Integrating geographic information systems, models, and visualization tools*, ed. Richard K. Brail and Richard E. Klosterman, 1–23. Redlands, Calif.: ESRI Press.

Koch, Tom. 2005. *Cartographies of disease: Maps, mapping, and medicine.* Redlands, Calif.: ESRI Press.

Kretzman, J., and J. McKnight. 1994. Building communities from the inside out: A path toward finding and mobilizing a community's assets. Evanston, Ill.: Center for Urban Affairs and Policy Research. Northwestern University.

Laguerre, Michel S. 2000. *The global ethnopolis: Chinatown, Japantown, and Manilatown in American society.* New York: St. Martin's Press.

Landis, John D. 2001. CUF, CUF II, and CURBA: A family of spatially explicit urban growth and land-use policy simulation models. In *Planning support systems: Integrating geographic information systems, models, and visualization tools*, ed. Richard K. Brail and Richard E. Klosterman, 157–200 Redlands, Calif.: ESRI Press.

Landis, John D., and Ming Zhang. 2000. Using GIS to improve urban activity and forecasting models: Three examples. In *Spatial models and GIS: New potential and new models*, eds. A. Stewart Fotheringham and Michael Wegener, 63–81. London: Taylor and Francis.

Le Gales, Patrick. 2002. *European cities: Social conflicts and governance.* Oxford, U.K.: Oxford University Press.

LeGates, Richard T. 2005. *Think globally, act regionally: GIS and data visualization for social science and public policy research.* Redlands, Calif.: ESRI Press.

LeGates, Richard T., and Frederic Stout, eds. 2003. *The city reader.* 3rd ed. London: Routledge.

Li, W. 1998. Anatomy of a new ethnic settlement: The Chinese ethnoburbs in Los Angeles. *Urban Studies* 35(3).

Light, Ivan. June 2002. Immigrant place entrepreneurs in Los Angeles, 1970–99. *International Journal of Urban and Regional Research* 26(2): 215–28.

Light, Ivan, and Steven J. Gold. 2000. *Ethnic economies.* San Diego: Academic Press.

Lin, Y. 1998. *Reconstructing Chinatown: Ethnic enclave, global change.* Minneapolis: University of Minnesota Press.

Logan, John R., Richard D. Alba, and Wenquan Zhang. 2002. Immigrant enclaves and ethnic communities in New York and Los Angeles. *American Sociological Review* vol. 67: 299–322.

Logan, John R., and Wenquan Zhang. 2004. Identifying ethnic neighborhoods with census data: Group concentration and spatial clustering. In *Spatially integrated social science*, ed. Michael F. Goodchild and Donald G. Janelle, 113–26. New York: Oxford University Press.

Longley, Paul A., Michael F. Goodchild, David J. Maguire, and David W. Rhind. 2005. *Geographic information systems and science.* 2nd ed. Chichester, West Sussex, England: John Wiley and Sons, Ltd.

Lynch, Kevin. 1960. *The image of the city.* Cambridge, Mass.: The MIT Press.

Mahler, S. J. 1995. *Salvadorans in suburbia: Symbiosis and conflict.* Boston: Allyn and Bacon.

Marcuse, Peter, and Ronald van Kempen, eds. 2000. *Globalizing cities: A new spatial order?* Oxford, U.K.: Blackwell.

Massey, Douglas S. 1985. Ethnic residential segregation: A theoretical and empirical review. *Sociology and Social Research* 69:315–50.

Massey, Douglas S., and Nancy A. Denton. 1993. *American apartheid: Segregation and the making of the underclass.* Cambridge, Mass.: Harvard University Press.

———. 1988. The dimensions of residential segregation. *Social Forces* 67:281–315.

McHarg, Ian. 1969. *Design with nature.* Garden city: Doubleday and Company.

Monmonier, M. 1996. *How to lie with maps.* 2nd ed. Chicago: University of Chicago Press.

Moser, Caroline. 1998. The asset vulnerability framework: Reassessing urban poverty reduction strategies. *World Development* 26(1): 1–19.

Musterd, Sako, and Rinus Deurloo. 2002. Unstable immigrant concentrations in Amsterdam: Spatial segregation and integration of newcomers. *Housing Studies* 17(3): 487–503.

Musterd, Sako, and Wim Ostendorf. 2003. Understanding segregation in the metropolitan area of Amsterdam. In *Amsterdam human capital*, eds. Sako Musterd and Willem Salet, 181–197. Amsterdam: Amsterdam University Press.

Myers, Dowell. 1992. *Analysis with local census data: Portraits of change.* Boston: Academic Press, Inc.

———. 1999. Demographic dynamism and metropolitan change: Comparing Los Angeles, New York, Chicago, and Washington, D.C. *Housing Policy Debate.* 10(4): 919–54.

NCGIA. 2000. *The NCGIA core curriculum in GIScience.* www.ncgia.ucsb.edu/education/ curricula/giscc.

Nedovic-Budic, Zorica. 1999. Evaluating the effects of GIS technology: Review of methods. *Journal of Planning Literature* 13(3): 284–95.

———. 2000. Geographic information science implications for urban and regional planning. *URISA Journal* 12(2): 81–93.

Newton, James. 2001. Urban indicators and the management of cities. In *Cities databook: Urban indicators for managing cities*, eds. S. Matthew Westfall and Victoria A. de Villa. Manila, Philippines: Asian Development Bank.

Nishikawa, Nancy. 2003. Survey methods for planners. In *The planner's use of information.* 2nd ed., ed. Hemalata C. Dandekar, 51–78. Chicago, Ill.: Planners Press, American Planning Association.

Nyerges, T. L., and R. G. Golledge. November 1997. NCGIA core curriculum in GIS. National Center for Geographic Information and Analysis, University of California, Santa Barbara, Unit 007. www.ncgia.ucsb.edu/giscc/units/u007/u007.html.

O'Looney, John. 2000. *Beyond maps: GIS and decision making in local government.* Redlands, Calif.; ESRI Press.

Ong, Aihwa. 1999. *Flexible citizenship: The cultural logics of transnationality.* Durham, N.C.: Duke University Press.

Openshaw, Stan. 1984. *The modifiable areal unit problem: Concepts and techniques in modern geography 38.* Norwich, U.K.: GeoBooks.

Orfield, Myron. 2002. *American metropolitics: The new suburban reality.* Washington, D.C.: Brookings Institution Press.

Ormsby, Tim, Eileen Napoleon, Robert Burke, Carolyn Groessl, and Laura Feaster. 2004. *Getting to know ArcGIS desktop.* 2nd ed. Redlands, Calif.: ESRI Press.

Painter, Gary, Lihong Yang, and Zhou Yu. 2003. Heterogeneity in Asian American home-ownership: The impact of household endowments and immigrant status. *Urban Studies* 40(3): 505–30.

Pamuk Ayse. 1991. *Housing in developing countries: A select bibliography and field statement.* CPL Bibliography 273. Chicago: Council of Planning Librarians.

———. 1994. Housing production and transactions in developing countries: Do formal rule-systems matter? PhD diss., University of California, Berkeley.

———. 1996. Convergence trends in formal and informal housing markets: The case of Turkey. *Journal of Planning Education and Research* 16(2): 103–13.

———. 2000. Informal institutional arrangements in credit, land markets, and infrastructure delivery in Trinidad. *International Journal of Urban and Regional Research* 24(2): 379–96.

———. 2001. Tools for a land and housing market diagnosis. In *The challenge of urban government: Policies and practices*, eds. by Maria Emilia Friere and Richard Stren, 253–67. Toronto and Washington, D.C.: Centre for Urban and Community Studies, University of Toronto and the World Bank Institute.

———. January 2003. *Children in poverty in San Francisco.* Prepared for the San Francisco Head Start Program. Public Research Institute, SFSU.

———. 2004. Geography of immigrant clusters in global cities: A case study of San Francisco, 2000. *International Journal of Urban and Regional Research* 24(2): 379–96

Pamuk Ayse, and David E. Dowall. 1998. The price of land for housing in Trinidad: Implications for affordability. *Urban Studies* 35(2): 285–99.

Pamuk, Ayse, and Paulo Fernando A. Cavallieri. 1998. Alleviating urban poverty in a global city: New trends in upgrading Rio-de-Janeiro's favelas. *Habitat International* 22(4):449–62 [Erratum 23(3): 427–29, 1999].

Parker, Cheryl, and Amelita Pascual. 2002. A voice that could not be ignored: Community GIS and gentrification battles in San Francisco. In *Community participation and geographic information systems*, eds. William J. Craig, Trevor M. Harris, and Daniel Weiner, 55–64. London: Taylor and Francis.

Peters, Alan, and Heather MacDonald. 2004. *Unlocking the census with GIS.* Redlands, Calif.: ESRI Press.

Pincetl, Stephanie. 1996. Immigrants and redevelopment plans in Paris, France: Urban planning, equity, and environmental justice. *Urban Geography* 17(5): 440–55.

Portes, Alejandro, ed. 1995. *The economic sociology of immigration: Essays on networks, ethnicity, and entrepreneurship.* New York: Russell Sage Foundation.

Portes, Alejandro, and Julia Sensenbrenner. 1993. Embeddedness and immigration: Notes on the social determinants of economic action. *American Journal of Sociology* 98(6): 1320–50.

Portes, Alejandro, and Ruben G. Rumbaut. 1996. *Immigrant America: A portrait.* 2nd ed. Berkeley: University of California Press.

Queralt, Magaly, and Ann Dryden Witte. 1998. A map for you? Geographic information systems in the social services. *Social Work* 43(5): 455–69.

———. December 1999. Estimating the unmet need for services: A middling approach. *Social Service Review,* 524–59.

Reed, Deborah, and Amanda Bailey. November 2002. California's young children: Demographic, social, and economic conditions. In *California counts: Population trends and profiles.* San Francisco: Public Policy Institute of California.

Reed, Deborah, and R. Van Swearingen. November 2001. Poverty in California: Levels, Trends, and Demographic Dimension. In *California Counts,* vol.3, no. 3. San Francisco: Public Policy Institute of California.

Rifkin, Jeremy. 2004. *The European dream: How Europe's vision of the future is quietly eclipsing the American Dream.* New York: Jeremy P. Tarcher/Penguin.

Rubin, Victor. 1998. The roles of universities in community-building initiatives. *Journal of Planning Education and Research* 17(4): 302–11.

Samers, M. June 2002. Immigration and the global city hypothesis: Towards an alternative research agenda. *International Journal of Urban and Regional Research* 26(2): 389–402.

Sanjek, Roger. 1998. *The future of us all: Race and neighborhood politics in New York City.* Ithaca: Cornell University Press.

Sanyal, Bishwapriya, ed. 1990. *Breaking the boundaries: A one-world approach to planning education.* New York: Plenum Press.

Sassen, Saskia. 1991. *The global city: New York, London, Tokyo.* Princeton, N.J.: Princeton University Press.

———. 1998. *Globalization and its discontents: Essays on the new mobility of people and money.* New York: The New Press.

Sawicki, David S., and William J. Craig. 1996. The democratization of data: Bridging the gap for community groups. *Journal of the American Planning Association* 62(4): 512–23.

Saxenian, AnnaLee. 2002. *Local and global networks of immigrant professionals in Silicon Valley.* San Francisco: Public Policy Institute of California.

Schill, Michael H., S. Friedman, E. Rosenbaum. 1998. The housing condition of immigrants in New York City. *Journal of Housing Research* 9(2): 201–35.

Scott, Allen. ed. 2002. *Global city-regions: Trends, theory, policy.* New York: Oxford University Press.

Sen, Amartya. 1999. *Development as freedom.* New York: Alfred A. Knopf.

Shen, Qing. 2004. Updating spatial perspectives and analytical frameworks in urban research. In *Spatially integrated social science,* eds. Michael F. Goodchild and Donald G. Janelle, 263–79. New York: Oxford University Press.

Singer, Audrey. February 2004. The rise of new immigrant gateways. The Living Cities Census Series. Washington, D.C.: Center on Urban and Metropolitan Policy, The Brookings Institution.

Slocum, Terry A., Robert B. McMaster, Fritz C. Kessler, and Hugh H. Howard. 2005. *Thematic cartography and geographic visualization.* 2nd ed. Upper Saddle River, N.J.: Pearson, Prentice Hall.

Smith, Michael Peter. 2001. *Transnational urbanism: Locating globalization.* Malden, Mass.: Blackwell.

Solnit, Rebecca, and Susan Schwartzenberg. 2000. *Hollow city: The seige of San Francisco and the crisis of American urbanism.* London: Verso.

Stowers, Genie N. L. 1999. Becoming cyberactive: State and local governments on the World Wide Web. *Government Information Quarterly* 16(2): 111–27.

Takaki, Ronald. 1998. *Strangers from a different shore: A history of Asian Americans.* Revised and updated edition. Boston: Little, Brown, and Company.

Talen, Emily. 2000. Bottom-up GIS: A new tool for individual and group expression in participatory planning. *Journal of American Planning Association* 66(3): 279–94.

The New York Times. 2003. From Philippines, with scrubs: How one ethnic group came to dominate nursing.

Tufte, Edward R. 1983. *The visual display of quantitative information.* Cheshire, Connecticut: Graphics Press.

Turner, John F. C. 1977. *Housing by people: Towards automony in building environments.* New York: Pantheon Books.

Turner, M. A., and F. Skidmore. September 1999. Mortgage lending discrimination: A review of existing evidence. Washington, D.C.: The Urban Institute.

UNCHS and the World Bank. 1992. The housing indicators program extensive survey. Part II: Indicator modules and worksheets update and revisions. Washington, D.C.: World Bank.

UNICEF. 2001. *United Nations convention on the rights of the child.* November 20, 1989. www.unicef.org/crc/fulltext.htm.

United Nations. 1992. The Rio declaration on environment and development: Report of the United Nations Conference on Environment and Development. Rio de Janeiro: Brazil. June 3–14.

United Nations Centre for Human Settlements (HABITAT). 2001. *Cities in a globalizing world: Global report on Human Settlements 2001.* London: Earthscan.

United Nations Centre for Human Settlements (UNCHS). 1988. Global strategy for shelter for the year 2000. HS/C/11/3. Nairobi, Kenya: UNCHS.

———. 1998. Global Urban Indicators Database 2. www.unchs.org/programmes/guo/guo_indicators.asp.

United Nations Development Programme (UNDP). 2003. *Human development report 200. Millennium development goals: A compact among nations to end human poverty.* New York: Oxford University Press. hdr.undp.org/reports/global/2003.

University Consortium for Geographic Information Science. June 2003. The Strawman report: Development of model undergraduate curricula for geographic information science and technology. Task Force on the Development of Model Undergraduate Curricula. www.ucgis.org.

U.S. Census Bureau. December 2001. Profile of the foreign-born population in the United States: 2000. Current Population Reports, Special Studies, P23-206. www.census.gov.

U.S. Census Bureau. September 2001. Age: 2000. Census 2000 Brief. www.census.gov.

U.S. Census Bureau. John Iceland, and Daniel. H. Weinberg with Erika Steinmetz. August 2002. *Racial and ethnic residential segregation in the United States: 1980–2000.* Census 2000 Special Reports. CENSR-3. www.census.gov.

U.S. Department of Housing and Urban Development (HUD). www.hud.gov/local/sfc/sfcfmrca.html.

Waldinger, Roger. 2002. The immigrant niche in global city-regions: Concept, patterns, controversy. In *Global city-regions: Trends, theory, policy,* ed. Allen J. Scott, 299–322. Oxford, U.K.: Oxford University Press.

Waldinger, Roger, and M. Bozorgmehr, eds. 1996. *Ethnic Los Angeles.* New York: Russell Sage Foundation.

Walker, Richard. 1996. Another round of globalization in San Francisco. *Urban Geography* 17(1): 60–94.

Westfall, S. Matthew, and Victoria A. de Villa, eds. 2001. *Cities data book: Urban indicators for managing cities.* Manila, Philippines: Asian Development Bank.

Wilson, William Julius. 1987. *The truly disadvantaged: The inner city, the underclass, and public policy.* Chicago: The University of Chicago Press.

Wong, B. P. 1998. *Ethnicity and entrepreneurship: The new Chinese immigrants in the San Francisco Bay Area.* Boston: Allyn and Bacon.

Wong, David W. S. 2003. Implementing spatial segregation measures in GIS. *Computers, environment and urban systems* 27:53–70.

Wood, J. 1997. Vietnamese American place making in Northern Virginia. *The Geographical Review* 87(1): 58–72.

Yen, Maria, and Grace York. 2003. Information from secondary sources. In *The planner's use of information.* 2nd ed., ed. Hemalata C. Dandekar, 81–122. Chicago, Ill.: Planners Press, American Planning Association.

Zeiler, Michael. 1999. *Modeling our world: The ESRI guide to geodatabase design.* Redlands, Calif.: ESRI Press.

Zhou, Min. 1992. *Chinatown: The socio-economic potential of an urban enclave.* Philadelphia: Temple University Press.

Zigler, Edward, and Jeanette Valentine, eds. 1979. *Project Head Start: A legacy of the war on poverty.* New York: The Free Press.

Zigler, Edward, and Susan Muenchow. 1992. *Head Start: The inside story of America's most successful educational experiment.* New York: Basic Books.

Zook, Matthew A. 2000. The web of production: The economic geography of commercial Internet content production in the United States. *Environment and Planning* A 32: 411–26.

Data license agreement

Important:

Read carefully before opening the sealed media package.

ENVIRONMENTAL SYSTEMS RESEARCH INSTITUTE, INC. (ESRI), IS WILL-
ING TO LICENSE THE ENCLOSED DATA AND RELATED MATERIALS TO YOU
ONLY UPON THE CONDITION THAT YOU ACCEPT ALL OF THE TERMS AND
CONDITIONS CONTAINED IN THIS LICENSE AGREEMENT. PLEASE READ
THE TERMS AND CONDITIONS CAREFULLY BEFORE OPENING THE SEALED
MEDIA PACKAGE. BY OPENING THE SEALED MEDIA PACKAGE, YOU ARE
INDICATING YOUR ACCEPTANCE OF THE ESRI LICENSE AGREEMENT. IF
YOU DO NOT AGREE TO THE TERMS AND CONDITIONS AS STATED, THEN
ESRI IS UNWILLING TO LICENSE THE DATA AND RELATED MATERIALS TO
YOU. IN SUCH EVENT, YOU SHOULD RETURN THE MEDIA PACKAGE WITH
THE SEAL UNBROKEN AND ALL OTHER COMPONENTS TO ESRI.

ESRI License Agreement

This is a license agreement, and not an agreement for sale, between you (Licensee) and Environmental Systems Research Institute, Inc. (ESRI). This ESRI License Agreement (Agreement) gives Licensee certain limited rights to use the data and related materials (Data and Related Materials). All rights not specifically granted in this Agreement are reserved to ESRI and its Licensors.

Reservation of Ownership and Grant of License:
ESRI and its Licensors retain exclusive rights, title, and ownership to the copy of the Data and Related Materials licensed under this Agreement and, hereby, grant to Licensee a personal, nonexclusive, nontransferable, royalty-free, worldwide license to use the Data and Related Materials based on the terms and conditions of this Agreement. Licensee agrees to use reasonable effort to protect the Data and Related Materials from unauthorized use, reproduction, distribution, or publication.

Proprietary Rights and Copyright:
Licensee acknowledges that the Data and Related Materials are proprietary and confidential property of ESRI and its Licensors and are protected by United States copyright laws and applicable international copyright treaties and/or conventions.

Permitted Uses:
Licensee may install the Data and Related Materials onto permanent storage device(s) for Licensee's own internal use.
Licensee may make only one (1) copy of the original Data and Related Materials for archival purposes during the term of this Agreement unless the right to make additional copies is granted to Licensee in writing by ESRI.
Licensee may internally use the Data and Related Materials provided by ESRI for the stated purpose of GIS training and education.

Uses Not Permitted:
Licensee shall not sell, rent, lease, sublicense, lend, assign, time-share, or transfer, in whole or in part, or provide unlicensed Third Parties access to the Data and Related Materials or portions of the Data and Related Materials, any updates, or Licensee's rights under this Agreement. Licensee shall not remove or obscure any copyright or trademark notices of ESRI or its Licensors.

Term and Termination:
The license granted to Licensee by this Agreement shall commence upon the acceptance of this Agreement and shall continue until such time that Licensee elects in writing

to discontinue use of the Data or Related Materials and terminates this Agreement. The Agreement shall automatically terminate without notice if Licensee fails to comply with any provision of this Agreement. Licensee shall then return to ESRI the Data and Related Materials. The parties hereby agree that all provisions that operate to protect the rights of ESRI and its Licensors shall remain in force should breach occur.

Disclaimer of Warranty:

THE DATA AND RELATED MATERIALS CONTAINED HEREIN ARE PROVIDED "AS-IS," WITHOUT WARRANTY OF ANY KIND, EITHER EXPRESS OR IMPLIED, INCLUDING, BUT NOT LIMITED TO, THE IMPLIED WARRANTIES OF MER-CHANTABILITY, FITNESS FOR A PARTICULAR PURPOSE, OR NONINFRINGE-MENT. ESRI does not warrant that the Data and Related Materials will meet Licensee's needs or expectations, that the use of the Data and Related Materials will be uninterrupted, or that all nonconformities, defects, or errors can or will be corrected. ESRI is not inviting reliance on the Data or Related Materials for commercial planning or analysis purposes, and Licensee should always check actual data.

Data Disclaimer:

The Data used herein has been derived from actual spatial or tabular information. In some cases, ESRI has manipulated and applied certain assumptions, analyses, and opinions to the Data solely for educational training purposes. Assumptions, analyses, opinions applied, and actual outcomes may vary. Again, ESRI is not inviting reliance on this Data, and the Licensee should always verify actual Data and exercise their own professional judgment when interpreting any outcomes.

Limitation of Liability:

ESRI shall not be liable for direct, indirect, special, incidental, or consequential damages related to Licensee's use of the Data and Related Materials, even if ESRI is advised of the possibility of such damage.

No Implied Waivers:

No failure or delay by ESRI or its Licensors in enforcing any right or remedy under this Agreement shall be construed as a waiver of any future or other exercise of such right or remedy by ESRI or its Licensors.

Order for Precedence:

Any conflict between the terms of this Agreement and any FAR, DFAR, purchase order, or other terms shall be resolved in favor of the terms expressed in this Agreement, subject to the government's minimum rights unless agreed otherwise.

Export Regulation:

Licensee acknowledges that this Agreement and the performance thereof are subject to compliance with any and all applicable United States laws, regulations, or orders relating to the export of data thereto. Licensee agrees to comply with all laws, regulations, and orders of the United States in regard to any export of such technical data.

Severability:

If any provision(s) of this Agreement shall be held to be invalid, illegal, or unenforceable by a court or other tribunal of competent jurisdiction, the validity, legality, and enforceability of the remaining provisions shall not in any way be affected or impaired thereby.

Governing Law:

This Agreement, entered into in the County of San Bernardino, shall be construed and enforced in accordance with and be governed by the laws of the United States of America and the State of California without reference to conflict of laws principles. The parties hereby consent to the personal jurisdiction of the courts of this county and waive their rights to change venue.

Entire Agreement:

The parties agree that this Agreement constitutes the sole and entire agreement of the parties as to the matter set forth herein and supersedes any previous agreements, understandings, and arrangements between the parties relating hereto.

Data and exercises

Mapping Global Cities includes one CD containing the exercise data needed to perform the five exercises and self-directed project. This data takes up about 107 megabytes of hard-disk space. You will need a printer to print the exercises, which are contained on this CD in PDF format. You will need the latest version of Adobe Reader installed on your computer to open and read the exercises. To download a free version of Adobe Reader, go to *www.adobe.com*.

Installing the exercise data

Put the CD into your computer's CD drive.

Click the "Install Exercise Data for *Mapping Global Cities*" button, then follow the installation instructions and note the location of the data on your hard drive.

Using the "Typical" install option will install the exercise data to the directory C:\GISMethods.

Seven data files will be downloaded onto your hard drive:

Brazil_census
HS_raster
HS_vector
My_Work
Self_directed_project
SF_immigrant_clusters
WB_housing_join

Uninstalling the exercise data

To uninstall the exercise data from your computer, open your operating system's control panel and double-click the Add/Remove Programs icon. In the Add/Remove Programs dialog box, select the "*Mapping Global Cities*" entry to remove it.

Accessing the exercises

Click the "*Mapping Global Cities* Exercises" button. This will bring up the Mapping GlobalCities_Exercise.pdf file (5.61 MB). The file contains the following:

About the exercises
Exercise 1 Create a thematic map
Exercise 2 Spatialize nonspatial data
Exercise 3 Analyze vector data
Exercise 4 Analyze raster data
Exercise 5 Calculate new information
Self-directed project: Planning in the new global metropolis

Index

A

absolute locations, 96
absolute values, 65
accessibility, 85, 96
ACS (American Community Survey), 52
ADB (Asian Development Bank), 60
aerial photography, 26, 55, 61
Alba, Richard D., 112, 124
American Community Survey (ACS), 52
analysis
    cross-national data, 53
    cross-sectional data, 64
    multilayer, 40–42, 73, 89, 103
    point-in-polygon, 42
    proximity, 73, 83, 85–89, 101
    scale of, 28, 31
    single-layer, 37, 40
    spatial patterns, 43
    temporal data, 64, 132–133

Books from

ESRI Press

Advanced Spatial Analysis: The CASA Book of GIS *1-58948-073-2*
ArcGIS and the Digital City: A Hands-on Approach for Local Government *1-58948-074-0*
ArcView GIS Means Business *1-879102-51-X*
A System for Survival: GIS and Sustainable Development *1-58948-052-X*
A to Z GIS: An Illustrated Dictionary of Geographic Information Systems *1-58948-140-2*
Beyond Maps: GIS and Decision Making in Local Government *1-879102-79-X*
Cartographica Extraordinaire: The Historical Map Transformed *1-58948-044-9*
Cartographies of Disease: Maps, Mapping, and Medicine *1-58948-120-8*
Charting the Unknown: How Computer Mapping at Harvard Became GIS *1-58948-118-6*
Children Map the World: Selections from the Barbara Petchenik Children's World Map Competition *1-58948-125-9*
Community Geography: GIS in Action *1-58948-023-6*
Community Geography: GIS in Action Teacher's Guide *1-58948-051-1*
Confronting Catastrophe: A GIS Handbook *1-58948-040-6*
Conservation Geography: Case Studies in GIS, Computer Mapping, and Activism *1-58948-024-4*
Designing Better Maps: A Guide for GIS Users *1-58948-089-9*
Designing Geodatabases: Case Studies in GIS Data Modeling *1-58948-021-X*
Disaster Response: GIS for Public Safety *1-879102-88-9*
Extending ArcView GIS (version 3.x edition) *1-879102-05-6*
Fun with GPS *1-58948-087-2*
Getting to Know ArcGIS Desktop, Second Edition Updated for ArcGIS 9 *1-58948-083-X*
Getting to Know ArcObjects: Programming ArcGIS with VBA *1-58948-018-X*
Getting to Know ArcView GIS (version 3.x edition) *1-879102-46-3*
GIS and Land Records: The ArcGIS Parcel Data Model *1-58948-077-5*
GIS for Environmental Management *1-58948-142-9*
GIS for Everyone, Third Edition *1-58948-056-2*
GIS for Health Organizations *1-879102-65-X*
GIS for Landscape Architects *1-879102-64-1*
GIS for the Urban Environment *1-58948-082-1*
GIS for Water Management in Europe *1-58948-076-7*
GIS in Public Policy: Using Geographic Information for More Effective Government *1-879102-66-8*
GIS in Telecommunications *1-879102-86-2*
GIS Means Business, Volume II *1-58948-033-3*
GIS, Spatial Analysis, and Modeling *1-58948-130-5*
GIS Tutorial for Health *1-58948-148-8*
GIS Tutorial: Workbook for ArcView 9 *1-58948-127-5*
GIS Worlds: Creating Spatial Data Infrastructures *1-58948-122-4*
Hydrologic and Hydraulic Modeling Support with Geographic Information Systems *1-879102-80-3*

Continued on next page

When ordering, please mention book title and ISBN (number that follows each title)

Books from ESRI Press (continued)

Ask for ESRI Press titles at your local bookstore or order by calling 1-800-447-9778. You can also shop online at www.esri.com/esripress. Outside the United States, contact your local ESRI distributor.

ESRI Press titles are distributed to the trade by the following:

In North America, South America, Asia, and Australia:
Independent Publishers Group (IPG)
Telephone (United States): 1-800-888-4741 • Telephone (international): 312-337-0747
E-mail: frontdesk@ipgbook.com

In the United Kingdom, Europe, and the Middle East:
Transatlantic Publishers Group Ltd.
Telephone: 44 20 7373 2515 • Fax: 44 20 7244 1018 • E-mail: richard@tpgltd.co.uk

ESRI Press • 380 New York Street • Redlands, California 92373-8100 • www.esri.com/esripress